Cambridge Elements ≡

Elements in Global Urban History
edited by
Michael Goebel
Graduate Institute Geneva
Tracy Neumann
Wayne State University
Joseph Ben Prestel
Freie Universität Berlin

GLOBALIZING URBAN ENVIRONMENTAL HISTORY

Matthew Vitz
University of California

CAMBRIDGE
UNIVERSITY PRESS

Shaftesbury Road, Cambridge CB2 8EA, United Kingdom

One Liberty Plaza, 20th Floor, New York, NY 10006, USA

477 Williamstown Road, Port Melbourne, VIC 3207, Australia

314–321, 3rd Floor, Plot 3, Splendor Forum, Jasola District Centre,
New Delhi – 110025, India

103 Penang Road, #05–06/07, Visioncrest Commercial, Singapore 238467

Cambridge University Press is part of Cambridge University Press & Assessment,
a department of the University of Cambridge.

We share the University's mission to contribute to society through the pursuit of
education, learning and research at the highest international levels of excellence.

www.cambridge.org
Information on this title: www.cambridge.org/9781009475778

DOI: 10.1017/9781009400367

When citing this work, please include a reference to the DOI 10.1017/9781009400367

First published 2024

A catalogue record for this publication is available from the British Library.

ISBN 978-1-009-47577-8 Hardback
ISBN 978-1-009-40035-0 Paperback
ISSN 2632-3206 (online)
ISSN 2632-3192 (print)

Globalizing Urban Environmental History

Elements in Global Urban History

DOI: 10.1017/9781009400367
First published online: June 2024

Matthew Vitz
University of California

Author for correspondence: Matthew Vitz, mvitz@ucsd.edu

Abstract: *"Globalizing Urban Environmental History"* melds the methodological prescriptions of global urban history, the innovative methods of environmental history, and the interdisciplinary field of urban political ecology to trace the contours of a global urban environmental history. I argue that a global lens fixed on material, political, and cultural flows, movements, and connections – all of which were founded upon the structural integration of urban spaces through capitalist expansion and empire – sheds new light on the histories of specific urban-political ecologies, on the one hand, and large-scale urban patterns on the other. These patterns comprise shared urban-environmental imaginaries, strategies of environmental governance, and a global urban physical and cultural landscape stitched together by the adoption of fossil fuels.

Keywords: urban political ecology, urban environmental imaginary, diseases, petroleumscape, urban metabolism

ISBNs: 9781009475778 (HB), 9781009400350 (PB), 9781009400367 (OC)
ISSNs: 2632-3206 (online), 2632-3192 (print)

Contents

Introduction

Earthquakes are inherently local events. Rock masses shift in a specific location along a geological fault, sending seismic waves that can damage the built environment. And, when they occur near a major city, mass casualties sometimes result. Many of the most devastating earthquakes in world history, although not necessarily the most fatal, were those that have wrecked large metropolitan areas: San Francisco in 1906; Tokyo-Yokohama in 1923; Ashgabat, Turkmenistan, in 1948; Managua, Nicaragua, in 1972; Tangshan, China, in 1976; Mexico City in 1985; Kobe, Japan, in 1995; Port-au-Prince, Haiti, in 2010. Scholars of urban earthquakes tend to employ local and national registers to trace their destruction and impacts, as well as the process of rebuilding. They follow building codes and local planning, the class and racial disparities of earthquake damage, and grass-roots mobilization. Sometimes, major earthquakes are interpreted as watershed moments in national politics: for example, earthquakes in San Juan, Argentina, in 1944, Managua in 1972, and Mexico City in 1985 empowered popular movements and civil societies vis-à-vis authoritarian states (Buchenau and Johnson 2009; Healey 2011; Rodgers 2013).

Rarely are earthquakes, given their place-specific dynamics, understood in global-historical frameworks of connectivity and convergence. What would a global history of an urban earthquake look like? We might consider the global formation of earthquake science and earthquake-ready building codes or the global expertise driving rebuilding efforts, especially in cities throughout the Global South in the twentieth century (Coen 2013). We might explore the global dimensions of race- and class-based tensions – for example, the movement of people, animals, and diseases that stigmatized some peoples and neighborhoods as less worthy of reconstruction, or worse, as fit for removal. The 1906 San Francisco earthquake and fire, as historian Joanna Dyl (2017) has asserted, cannot be understood outside urban Chinese migrant subsistence practices and the racialized stigmas of Chinatown that the bubonic plague outbreak had reinforced among the urban elite several years before the quake. Certainly not all earthquakes have equally global dimensions; historical epoch matters. The first "global quake" may have been the Lisbon earthquake-tsunami-fire of 1755. It sparked perhaps the first internationally coordinated relief effort, and according to one historian, changed the course of the European Enlightenment (Molesky 2015). However, one might say that the nineteenth century inaugurated the era of the globalized quake when urban planning and development practice spread widely, the movement of people and the companion species (including diseases) they brought with them accelerated, global markets formed, and racist colonial ideologies circulated across diverse urban centers.

The way historians tend to study urban earthquakes mirrors the way urban environmental history writ large has taken shape over the past several decades. Urban historians often study nature in the city, circumscribed by the city's limits – what urban political ecologists David Wachsmuth and Hillary Angelo (2015) call "methodological cityism." Even when historians expand their spatial scale, they remain bound, generally, to the immediate hinterlands or the region, exploring topics such as suburbanization, capital flows, or "urban metabolisms" – the energy, water, waste, foods, as well as other material inputs and outputs, that flow between cities and wider metropolitan hinterlands (Cronon 1991; Rome 2001; Dagenais and Castonguay 2011; Needham 2014; Sellers 2015; Vitz 2018; Kim 2019). The emphases on place-making; the workings of local ecological processes; the peculiarities of municipal governance; and the concentrations of peoples who must be governed and provisioned – and who in turn make political claims to improve their lives – explain these more narrow geographical scales. The result has been a long list of city biographies and metropolitan histories, in addition to a smaller list of comparative histories that analyze environmental processes in two or more cities undergoing a similar transformation, such as industrialization (Platt 2005).

"Globalizing Urban Environmental History" is predicated on the notion that global patterns and connections have created what on the surface appear to be highly localized and specific urban environments. And, in turn, seemingly disconnected and localized urban-environmental conditions and processes help shape global history. By simultaneously zooming in on the idiosyncrasies of local urban ecologies and zooming out to discern connections, I outline what a global urban environmental history can look like. In this Element, I will argue that a global lens fixed on the material, political, and cultural flows, movements, and connections made possible by capitalist expansion and empire sheds new light on the histories of specific urban-political ecologies, on the one hand, and the large-scale material-ecological and political forces that produce wider urban patterns on the other. These patterns comprise shared urban-environmental imaginaries, strategies of environmental governance, and a global urban landscape stitched together by the adoption of fossil fuels.

Global history has reshaped the fields of urban and architectural history whose practitioners had cast their lens beyond the local urban form only superficially. When such historians studied the cities of the Global South, their conclusions were often implicitly comparative with a normative Euro-American model that revealed their urban sites as "lacking" in some important characteristic – legality, planning, industry, civil society, and so on – that European or North American metropolises had supposedly attained (Davis 2005; Robinson 2006; McFarlane 2010). They followed, in effect, the script of modernization theory whereby cities throughout the Global South were to be evaluated based on their "stages of development," a theory that derived from nineteenth-century colonialist ideology. Global urban historians, however, reject these approaches that stress urban difference and relegate non-Western cities to an inferior status. Instead, they draw on recent historical studies that highlight the mutual construction of European (metropolitan) and colonized spaces and cultures in order to delve more deeply into the variegated histories of "globalization." No one global urban history employs the same method; different geographic scopes and varied emphases on local, regional, and global spatial registers abound. The unifying thread of global urban history, however, is the study of the connective tissues that bind cities together: planning and architectural ideas; transnational urban political struggles and cultural movements; and the flows of materials, micro-organisms, commodities, finances, and people. In these histories, expanding the geographical scope of analysis reveals otherwise occluded patterns and con-nections that themselves become the subjects of study, the global phenomena that make and remake cities (Echenberg 2007; Nightingale 2012; Goebel 2015; Kwak 2015; Kenny and Madgin 2016; Sandoval Strausz and Kwak 2018). In other words, by zooming out to a global perspective and pinpointing causative global forces, urban historians explain more fully the histories of individual cities and groups of cities (Nightingale 2016). In this approach, cities become nodes of contact where the "local" and the "global" interact not as binaries but as co-constitutive forces (Tsing 2005; Sugrue 2018).

Apart from a number of histories of public health and medicine that follow epidemics across urban spaces, the nonhuman environmental realm rarely figures in this broader field of global urban history. Meanwhile, as previously mentioned, much urban-environmental history scholarship since the 1980s remains stuck in the particularities of local urban ecosystems, that is, of singularity and difference. This Element melds the methodological prescriptions of global urban history, the innovative methods of environmental history, and the interdisciplinary field of urban political ecology to trace the contours of a global urban environmental history. To do this, I identify connectivity, convergence, and divergence and center the historical agency of the nonhuman world, activated within particular urban practices and formations – global and otherwise (Nash 2005; Latour 2005; Bennett 2010; Walker 2011). The human and nonhuman realms of a city inter-twine to create the urban ecology, or the urban environment, terms I use inter-changeably. And I define these terms capaciously as the built environment and the urban technical networks that carry natural elements (water and energy, for example) in and out of cities; the labor activities that literally produce "nature" in cities; the plants, animals, micro-organisms, and biophysical processes within urban spaces; and the cultural imaginaries that represent urban nature.

Concepts and Method for a New Global Urban Environmental History

The sections that follow draw on decades of scholarship on political ecology, cities, and global history. Throughout I will employ several key methods and concepts from this literature that enrich our interpretation of historical urban ecologies as global phenomena. My objective here is to define and establish a clear and common understanding of them and show why they are useful for our purposes.

My approach to global urban history is grounded in the large-scale structural integration of the globe through two intertwined historical forces that ramped up in the nineteenth century: capitalism and imperialism. Capitalists increasingly relied on their state's territorial (colonial) expansion to extract and commercialize mineral and other resources and appropriate land to sustain their profits and thus sustain the capitalist system's inherent growth logic. European and North American imperial actors, in turn, justified territorial expansion and rule over foreign peoples through racist ideologies such as "the civilizing mission," "white man's burden," and other ideas that posited Native inferiority and European (and Euro-descendent) superiority. Working together, commercial and industrial capitalism and European and US-American imperialism linked urban political, cultural, and physical forms in new ways, producing simultaneously a convergence and a divergence of experiences. Scientific and planning ideas and the flows and movements of people, organisms, diseases, and commodities operated within these asymmetrical structural forces of integration. Meanwhile, nation-state consolidation across Western Europe, Latin America, and parts of East Asia, as well as nationalist movements across the colonized world – all of which were structurally interconnected through global ideologies of liberal capitalism and later Marxism – also frame the comparisons and connections I trace in this Element. Borrowing from Sebastian Conrad (2015), it is the structural integration of urban spaces across national and imperial borders that gives the flows and exchanges global historians like to study their causal force. This globalizing process of the urban form is the foundation of this Element. My emphasis on global structural integration, however, does not imply Eurocentric diffusionism. Instead, I underscore mutual interaction, exchange, and the synchronicity of urban change wherein multiple urban experiences, the global reverberations of local encounters, and large-scale patterns beyond a single nation are better comprehended.

In the Western imagination, cities have been understood as anti-nature, either artificial stains on a pristine nature or a bucolic countryside, or, more often, metonyms of technological prowess and progress that subjugates nature. Starting in the early twentieth century, urban ecologists and some environmentally minded planners began to explore the importance of nature in cities, as a set of elements to be properly governed, regulated, and cultivated to foster urban growth and preserve health. This thinking has culminated in ecological modernization prescriptions such as "green growth" and "smart cities" that dominate environmental planning today. However, several decades of scholarship by urban geographers and urban-environmental historians have countered this "apolitical urban ecology" that separates nature from social power and capitalist production. Their critical interrogation of urban ecologies has revolved around infrastructural politics, power relations, class and other forms of social conflict, and urban-environmental imaginaries (Gandy 2002; Heynen, Kaika, and Swyngedouw 2006; Heynen 2014; Heynen 2016; Simpson and Bagelman 2018; Cornea, Véron, and Zimmer 2017). Moreover, some of these studies transcend the confines of city boundaries to include the metropolitan, regional, or hinterland ecologies that become entangled in the process of urbanization – the infrastructural planning of cities, cultural representations and what urban political ecologists call, the "urban metabolism" (Swyngedouw 2004; Delgado Ramos 2015; Schmidt 2017; Coplen 2018)

Neil Brenner and Christian Schmid, who adopt Henri Lefebvre's understanding of a late twentieth-century "urban revolution," extend the urban metabolism metaphor. They contend that we are undergoing a period of "planetary urbanization" in which the whole world, even spaces long considered "rural," are becoming essentially urban because of their industrialized extractive systems of production and technical infrastructures (Lefebvre 2003; Brenner 2014). While urbanization has been an extraordinary social phenomenon across all six inhabited continents, it hardly makes sense to view all spaces enwrapped in urban metabolisms as themselves "urban." Alternatively, historian Chris Otter (2017) proposes that urban researchers employ the term "global technosphere" to denote these diverse built environments that are created through urbanization but whose social relations, politics, and culture are not reducible to it or defined exclusively by it. This global technosphere, I argue in Section 2, was made possible by the global energy transition from solar (water, wood, wind, muscle) to fossil energy, particularly the multiple uses of petroleum and the ease of its transport. Petroleum, as the lifeblood of a global energy metabolism, has allowed empires, nation-states, and capitalists to create new and interconnected urban spaces. I thus borrow Otter's ideas of globalized technical systems to explore the political, economic, cultural, and physical manifestations of an urban world made of and through petroleum, or what one urban scholar has called the "global urban petroleumscape" (Hein 2018).

This Element is not purely a top-down history of political and economic elites and technical experts (planners, public health officials, investors, and engineers) devising environmental governance strategies and large technical systems.

I remain attentive to the genealogies of popular resistance, citizenship claims and the obstacles to achieving them, and worker organizing. These often highly particular practices, while stemming from global patterns of environmental governance and energy metabolisms, cause variations across urban spaces. Thus, a global urban environmental history must simultaneously attend to the synchronous and patterned urban transformations made possible by colonial capitalist expansion, different racist regimes, and nation-state consolidation throughout the nineteenth and twentieth centuries, as well as the local idiosyncrasies that have made diverse urban-political ecologies. It is in this encounter, the frictions of the local and the global, that allow us to bring into sharper relief both the environmental histories of individual cities and the global patterns and connections that have made those cities what they are.

In sum, I make four major conceptual and methodological propositions to support this outline of a global urban environmental history. First, by the early nineteenth century, capitalism and empire, operating in tandem, as well as nation-state formation, enabled the types of flows, connections, and exchanges that bound previously discrete urban environments into a broadly similar historical process. Second, nonhuman nature – from diseases and animals to the energy resources that traverse cities – were constitutive forces of vast landscapes subjected to urbanization and regimes of urban governance enacted at regional and global scales. Third, the specific urban ecologies, the interacting set of social relations, the built environments, and the biophysical systems of a given city, were themselves interconnected. Urban ecologies tend to be studied in isolation, yet their historical dynamism is incomprehensible outside global circuits of ideas, people, and nonhuman nature such as diseases and resources situated within systems of production (both capitalist and socialist) and empires. In order to trace these connections, I position urban environmental history within histories of public health and the theoretical contributions of political ecology that understand urban metabolisms – the flows of materials and energy in and out of cities – across multiple spatial scales. I also track the technical experts who have reordered and tailored urban spaces and harnessed urban nature for human habitation. While the particularities of their interventions are unique to each city with their varying ecosystems, cultural tendencies, and state structures, the flow of ideas within circuits of empire helped generate the widespread political and cultural power of the urban expert. Fourth, the large-scale adoption of fossil fuels freed urban metabolisms of their regional boundaries. By the early twentieth century, fossil fuels, especially petroleum, not only made urban life tick but also linked cities together and cities to vast energy hinterlands, forming a global urban petroleumscape with immense political, ecological, and cultural consequences. In the conclusion, I address the challenges and opportunities this petroleumscape presents for the building of a decarbonized urban world in an age of climate destabilization.

1 Disease, Power, and the City: Global Urban Ecological Formations in the Age of Empire

During what historical epoch does it become meaningful to study urban environments as globally interconnected? Certainly, global connectivity did not emerge abruptly. There was no sudden switch that unleashed connections across oceans and administrative boundaries, nothing that demarcated a clear temporal boundary between a "before" and "after" globalization. Pre-modern and medieval historians have traced the "sporadic bursts" of spatial connectivity across empires and kingdoms, as well as the periods of recession and decompressions that disconnected cultures (Reinhard 2015). The spread of Islam in the medieval period created the conditions for the transfer of certain agricultural and irrigation techniques between the Middle East, Africa, and parts of Europe (Mikhail 2017). Trade between Europe and East Asia, in which the Middle East served as a conduit, also moved rodents across the Eurasian continent, transporting the bubonic plague that scourged Asian and European cities in the fourteenth century (Abu-Lughod 1991; Crossley 2008; Gitlin and Arenson 2013; Harrison 2013). A few exceptions notwithstanding, such wide-scaled spatial connections and exchanges tended to be concentrated in frontier zones, the interstices of empires. And, due to technological limitations in seafaring, those connections were rarely truly globe-trotting (Reinhard 2015). However, once seafaring technology, impelled by European commercial interests, improved, global urban-environmental connectivity intensified – first across the Atlantic. Spanish officials in New Spain, for example, brought European ideas about water management to Mexico City, with the purpose of draining the lake on which the city was built to protect urban properties and reclaim land for farming. This was not a simple story of idea transfer, however; the actual engineering of the urban waterscape in New Spain reflected a fusion of Indigenous and European knowledges and technologies (Candiani 2014). Spanish officials remade more than urban waterscapes. They changed the very foundation of urbanism in their colonial possessions from Manila and Mexico City to Lima by introducing grid road patterns and designing central squares reserved for Spanish settlement while Native peoples were relegated to the peripheries (Kagan 2000). The European settlers of North America, who did not rely on Native labor and governance traditions to support the colonial project, expropriated Indigenous lands outright and more systematically introduced to their towns and cities Europe's "portmanteau biota" (the term Alfred Crosby (2004) gives to the species Europeans brought with them). Wherever they went, Europeans sought to tailor their new urban sites to what they were familiar with back in Europe – their built environment and the plants and animals they used for transport and sustenance (Cronon 1983; Cleary 1997; Crosby 2004; Klingle 2007; Simpson 2022). On the other side of the Atlantic, Ottoman trade linked Cairo's ecosystem – its plants, animals, and micro-organisms – to a larger Mediterranean world (Mikhail 2012). Ocean-traversing empires of the seventeenth and eighteenth centuries generated new global connections that reshaped urban environments and spatial governance.

Urban-environmental connectivity intensified further starting in the early nineteenth century because of coal-fired capitalist industrialization and another burst of European imperialism in Asia and Africa. Textile manufacturing, increasingly powered by coal, spurred colonial trade in raw cotton, finished textiles, sugar, tea, and other commodities linking port cities and other entrepots such as Bombay, Madras, Calcutta, Hong Kong, Manila, Singapore, Hanoi, Havana, and New Orleans to metropolitan hubs like Liverpool, New York, Le Havre, and London. This trade between urban nodes fostered the biological integration of the globe. Diseases such as the bubonic plague, cholera, and yellow fever transmitted through either human contact or animal vectors, moved readily from port to port on board commercial (and military) ships.

Commerce created broadly similar levels of urban density across imperial port cities. Large numbers of workers settled in closely packed quarters near the warehouses and docks that harbored disease. By the 1830s, Liverpool's harbor teemed with ships, while workers – mostly Irish – toiled onshore loading and unloading bales of cotton between ship, warehouse, and train for a miserly wage (Beckert 2014). Similarly, in cities such as Bombay, Hong Kong, and Hanoi, a floating population of rural migrants seeking work in the bustling colonial ports lived in cramped, service-deficient, and substandard housing adjacent to port infrastructure.

For the *Aedes aegypti* mosquito, the vector of yellow fever, the warmth and humidity of commercial ships carrying sugar, and their ample supplies of fresh water, made for ideal long-distant vehicles for disease transmission, even occasionally into temperate cities like Philadelphia. Urban construction sites and docks, as well as warehouses full of barrels and other containers where rainwater accumulated, also made for ideal breeding grounds. And, as the sugar economy brought thousands of potentially unimmune merchants, enslaved workers, and soldiers to these ports, mosquitoes had ample means to spread the virus, known as "sailor's disease" throughout the French West Indies and as "black vomit" in the Hispanic Caribbean. "Ships, in effect were super-vectors," writes J.R. McNeill, and "ports . . . were super-hosts, providing warm welcomes for mosquito and virus alike" (McNeil 2010: 51–2). The same could be said of the plague-carrying fleas of the Norway rat, which found abundant habitat aboard ships crossing seas and oceans and in warehouses, and which easily jumped to the rat populations of adjacent worker neighborhoods (Echenberg 2007; Chhabria 2019; Webster 2021). The bacteria *Vibrio cholerae* (cholera), mostly dormant prior to the densification of colonial urban life, proliferated in the fast-growing slums of British India, and trade infrastructure brought the disease to Britain in 1831 where it tore through Liverpool's poorly serviced slums (Gill, Burrell, and Brown 2001). Colonial commerce and its unintentional companions, port infrastructures, as well as the growing urban congestion associated with trans-imperial trade, massively scaled up the global urban-ecological nexus.

Urban environments became not only interconnected biophysical formations but also, because of the rise of shared regimes of modern governance across nation-states and colonial possessions, interconnected sites of regulatory practice and intervention. The urban ecologies that arose through Western colonialism and early industrial capitalism raised a fundamental question of governance among elites: How would states – whether liberal republican, monarchical, or colonial – address the basic infrastructural and biological imperatives of city building? The answers to this urban question, in effect, animated modern state power. A new and empowered technical and scientific elite devised and circulated a set of representations about the relationship between cities and nature and between urban inhabitants and their health in inter-imperial travel, scientific publications, global sanitary conferences, and the intellectual exchanges of municipal governments. Within municipal, national, and colonial administrative units, these experts aimed to mitigate perceived environmental threats and transform urban spaces under the civilizing impulse that gripped nineteenth-century elites. They were charged with controlling, channeling, and tapping water; separating "bad" from "good" water; managing diseased environments and, later, diseased bodies; and controlling urban spaces deemed unruly and unhealthy through technical interventions and surveillance, marginalizing, in the process, opposing views of insalubrity. Urban environments were deemed increasingly knowable and governable, subjected to a strikingly portable set of interventions by government officials and technical experts. I call these shared representations, borne within the dual and intersecting process of imperial expansion and nation-state formation, the global urban-environmental imaginary. And, their repertoire of interventions – drainage and sanitary infrastructure, public health interventions, segregation, and urban forestry – stemmed from this environmental imaginary.

By placing in conversation a wide range of histories of nineteenth- and early twentieth-century public health, medicine, and cities and considering patterns of convergence and processes of divergence, it is possible to draw new conclusions about the global form of environmental governance, the racial hierarchies within urban-political ecologies, and the experiences of diverse urban populations inhabiting those new spaces. Although state officials attempted to "blackbox" their practices in the apolitical realm of the "technical," outside both social discord and nonhuman forces, those same practices operated through specific racial hierarchies inherent to colonialism, class relations, and the workings of nonhuman nature. Indeed, their practices helped establish those same categories (Joyce 2003). Nonhuman nature "spoke back," activated through the same interventions that intended to control it. Likewise, nonelite urban populations across colonial and metropolitan spaces shaped environmental governance and made their own urban spaces through revolt, negotiation, and adaptation.

The Sanitary Idea

In Western thought, the city has held positive associations with citizenship, and by the modern period, with enlightenment, progress, and civilization itself. These positive associations always had their referential opposite: ignorance and superstition, backwardness and barbarism. Western elites – state officials, capitalists, technical experts – feared these undersides would tarnish their bastions of civilization and refute their claims to modernity. Their notions of what counted as urban civilization and what counted as barbarism during the nineteenth century had much to do with a city's ability to conquer and harness the natural world, including water, forests, and the climatic and biochemical processes believed to produce disease.

It is beyond the scope of this section to thoroughly explore the interrelated social, cultural, and political processes that drove this impetus to separate the urban from the natural. One might trace its lineages within the Greco-Roman tradition or the rise of Christianity – perhaps all the way back to the invention of agriculture. More recent intellectual developments during the Scientific Revolution and the European Enlightenment, which established binaries of subject/object, culture/nature, and civilization/barbarism, were the more proximate causes of this new urban-environmental imagination. And, these intellectual developments incubated within Europe's colonization of the Americas and its commercial and imperial ventures in Africa and Asia. Commercial capitalism, in particular, induced investors and the scientists they employed to treat nature as a bundle of resources to be exploited and managed for the pursuit of profit. And cities, as cradles of capital accumulation and representations of imperial power, served to exemplify this mastery over nature, the equivalent of civilization itself. Yet, commercial (and later industrial) capitalism, and the imperial linkages through which it thrived, rendered cities more interwoven with an oft-unwieldy, and potentially harmful, urban nature. It was this dialectical relationship between intended mastery and control, on the one hand, and the biophysical forces and diverse social practices enacted through colonial capitalism, on the other, that made urban-environmental governance a global phenomenon. The first instantiation of this global form of governance was "sanitarianism."

In the nineteenth century, concepts like civilization and citizenship became more universal by virtue of the structural integration of the globe – the simultaneous processes of nation-state formation, capitalist expansion, and imperialism (Hill 2013). Sanitarianism – a technical and scientific conviction that joined epidemiology, public health interventions, urban planning, and hydraulic engineering – was another key global concept. And, similar to these other ideas, sanitarianism did not have a clear point of origin in Western Europe, as the story is traditionally told. Historians generally date modern sanitarianism to the early nineteenth-century work of the English physician and reformer Edwin Chadwick, who subscribed to the idea that disease was caused by noxious air (miasma theory). And, to be sure, Chadwickian ideas of urban sanitation, furthered by the reach of the British Empire, prevailed in many cities around the world by the 1850s. However, recent work in the history of global public health has traced the multiple origins and multidirectional formation of sanitarianism between colony and metropole and across metropolitan centers. As historian Jim Downs has argued, many of the key epidemiological presuppositions that underpinned the sanitary idea, indeed Chadwick's own theories, derived from studies conducted in colonial spaces and upon subject populations such as the enslaved and the imprisoned. It also bears mentioning that Europeans rediscovered Hippocrates' environmental epidemiology through Arabic texts and the Ottoman Empire's dealings with the plague (Varlik 2013; Downs 2021).

While Downs demonstrates the movement of ideas from colony to metropole, other historians have documented the ways sanitarianism assumed different forms in different contexts. Some of these adaptations even traveled from colonial and non-Euro-American contexts to metropolitan spaces (Peckham and Pomfret 2013). European and US-American naturalists, doctors, and travelers sought explanations for the apparent backwardness of the tropics and its epidemic maladies. Miasmas were everywhere, many believed, but the humid and hot conditions of the tropics weakened the human condition, making the tropics ideal places for disease, especially malaria and yellow fever. In the second half of the nineteenth century, Brazilian doctors challenged this notion of radical tropicality – the idea that the Brazilian tropics were innately diseased and backward – and argued that with the right sanitation measures amenable to the tropical environment, Brazil's urban populations could be improved and cured of chronic illness. These ideas came to prevail in turn-of-the-century discourse on tropical medicine around the world (Peard 1999).

Social relations at the local level, different social actors, state budgets and powers of surveillance, and the contingencies of nature molded how sanitation played out in specific locations. That is to say, this is not strictly a history of scientific or technical convergence, even if urban authorities on opposite ends of the world did often replicate interventions and share scientific knowledge. What urban elites held in common, however, was the strong conviction that the urban environment, in one way or another, needed to be transformed and populations improved. Rather than homogeneity and convergence of all aspects of knowledge, policy, and intervention, "public health" and "sanitation" were increasingly uttered everywhere to invoke a set of shared beliefs and convictions about who could hold knowledge about disease and disease prevention and who could intervene, how and where those interventions would take place, and who would be targeted.

The ideas of Chadwick and his acolytes during the first half of the century exemplified the emerging urban-environmental imaginary first known as sanitarianism. In their theory of disease, climatological conditions and putrefying organic waste, especially from unhealthy and stagnant waters, conspired to produce illness-causing miasmas. Doctors and other sanitary authorities also highlighted diseases caused by filth and cramped living quarters where poor ventilation made people more susceptible to miasmas. The Chadwickian urban-environmental paradigm, with its focus on general filth and local miasmas, superseded other ideas about the causal relation between disease and personal dispositions as well as general atmospheric patterns that had coexisted with miasmatic notions through the 1840s (Zeheter 2015). For an important moment in global urban history, Chadwickian miasma theory also tipped the balance of sanitary thought away from contagionism – the belief that disease could spread from person to person – that had legitimized the practice of quarantining of ships and, sometimes, entire neighborhoods (as had happened in the first bubonic plague in the 1340s). Even in France, a bulwark of contagionist theory, miasmatic theories gained an important following (Rabinow 1985). Regardless, the two theories were not dichotomous. Hybrid understandings such as "miasmatic contagionism" circulated widely, and nearly everyone agreed that Chadwick's proposed technical interventions – the construction of integrated sewerage and water supply systems and waste management – needed to be implemented.

The impulse to construct the sanitary city dovetailed with republican and colonial state-building – what scholars, drawing on Foucault, call "bio-power": the state's knowledge, management, and biological reproduction of its populations

(Joyce 2003; Chatterjee 2004; Pande 2010; Peckham and Pomfret 2013). Sanitarianism conferred power on the doctor, the administrator, and the engineer, solidifying their place among the state's technical elite. Meanwhile, governments expanded their role in society through the proliferation of technical systems. Such systems, in effect, helped form the modern state – whether monarchical, republican, or colonial.

The sanitary city involved more than state capacity, epidemiological theories, and engineering decisions. The technical systems and related medical interventions helped conjure a shared political culture of civilization. As Maria Kaika explains in *City of Flows* (2005), urban elites – engineers, city officials, doctors, and investor classes – harnessed sanitary infrastructure to their discursive and symbolic project of Western civilization. The control of urban water served as a vehicle for bourgeois and Western progress: moral rectitude and superiority became defined through ready access to "good" water flowing into the private home and the capacity to expel the "bad" water through hidden technical infrastructure (Sennett 1996; Kaika 2005; Nightingale 2022). Notions of liberal bourgeois domestic propriety, with clear private/public distinctions, rested on the water flowing through these technical infrastructures that guaranteed the healthy circulatory regime of a city, which many experts compared to biological organisms with their own metabolisms (Joyce 2003).

Chadwickian-influenced sanitation spread across colonial, metropolitan, and national spaces from the 1840s into the 1880s. Global forces helped to facilitate their adoption in otherwise culturally distinct areas of the world. First, the idea of "Western civilization" was constructed in the crucible of empire, through a historical association between European progress and ancient Greco-Roman societies and their wisdom in matters of politics, culture, and science. And, the environmental theory of disease had a strong heritage in Ancient Greece, from Hippocrates to Aristotle, where water, humidity, and humoral balance explained health. Second, while states had already assumed the task of re-engineering aquatic rural landscapes for profitable agricultural enterprises, theories of sanitation summoned the problems of urban health and planning that could only be resolved through the technical authority of the urban engineer, who would, in turn, bolster the legitimacy of governing authorities. These authorities were as likely to be municipal as national, and discussions about sanitary governance took place between not only colony and metropole but also across municipalities, in what two historians have labeled "municipal internationalism" (Saunier and Ewen 2008). Third, the profits generated by global commerce made the hyper-local environmental theory of disease more appealing to British elites and a wide range of authorities. It was politically convenient to locate the epidemics of typhoid and cholera in local miasmatic environments that could be ameliorated through technical systems rather than in the movement of people and goods upon which the whole global colonial order rested. Fourth, the appeal of sanitation also crossed ideological divides. For many elites, its appeal derived from what it promised not to challenge: the social relations of production and the coalescing class relations under commercial and industrial capitalism, particularly in Northern Europe. For some doctors and middle-class reformers of a more radical bent, sanitary reforms in neighborhoods and workplaces to promote health were critical to addressing the structural conditions of poverty and urban inequality. Thus, sanitarianism appealed to Progressive reformers of the Settlement projects of Chicago and socialist doctors such as Henry Sigerist alike (Fee and Brown 1997; Washington 2005; Browning 2022). Nonetheless, the prevailing current of sanitarianism, as progressive as it may have appeared to its contemporaries – bridging class divides and embodying the universal spirit of liberal and utilitarian government – largely ignored broader structural questions of poverty and working conditions (Joyce 2003; Molina 2006). State leaders could, therefore, flex their superior technical capacity, pronounce their association with a long lineage of Western civilization dating back to the Romans, and appeal to the masses of the city without interfering in commerce or industrial production.

The rise of bacteriology and the germ theory of disease in the 1880s and 1890s altered key aspects of the urban-environmental imaginary, and its attendant interventions, without remaking them entirely. Miasma-informed public health interventions persisted globally – limewashing walls, combatting filth on city streets, flushing carbolic acid down drains, and draining waterways – despite the mounting evidence against the environmental theory of disease. The metaphor of "seed and soil," the former as the agent of illness and the latter as the environmental conditions in which it thrives, became popularized. The rise of bacteriology, to be sure, gave substantial institutional and cultural power to the physicians and doctor-led public health boards who were charged with identifying and isolating bacteria and viruses and treating diseased bodies (Duffy 1990; Gilbert 2002). For the most part, however, bacteriology furthered the engineering imperative to supply clean water and evacuate dirty water, and, as several historians have asserted for the United States and Britain, could sustain a type of social environmentalism around housing reform (Platt 2005; Washington 2005; Browning 2022). Germ theory also sustained the conquest paradigm. Rather than unwieldy, putatively diseased environments (both tropical and temperate), the new battlefield was the micro-organism upon which modern medicine, in conjunction with the immune system, was tasked with obliterating (Nash 2006; Patel and Marya 2021).

Bacteriology had a more decisive effect on changing the ways disease was racialized. Whereas many of those subscribing to the environmental theory held that disease and mortality were less a personal or racial failing and more a result of environmental conditions, these ideas co-existed with elite metropolitan views of colonized peoples, and even their own poorer national counterparts, as morally and culturally backward. Meanwhile, the practitioners of tropical medicine, which borrowed much from miasmatic theories, often deployed tropical climate as a proxy for racial inferiority. Nonetheless, while the tropical climate could not be fundamentally changed, their focus on the environment disallowed more racist views. Bacteriology, however, centered personal hygiene and the human body within the urban-environmental gaze. And, Social Darwinism along with the new science of genetics, both of which provided a supposedly scientific basis for a hierarchy of civilizations and races, made this new body-fixated sanitation more fertile ground for racist practices (Browning 2022). Warwick Anderson traces the way racialization and bacteriology coincided in the American-controlled Philippines. Whereas the environmental theory of disease rendered tropical spaces unhealthy but potentially improvable with the correct environmental interventions, germ theory mixed with emerging scientific racism to cast Native peoples as innately prone to disease and averse to practices such as handwashing and personal hygiene (Anderson 2006; Legg 2013).

The structural forces of commercial capitalism, colonialism, and state building during the nineteenth century conjured an urban environment that shared similar characteristics across urban spaces. A wide assortment of sanitarians and state officials saw their urban spaces as disease-ridden, disordered, and full of corrupted and immoral poor people, and in need of proper environmental interventions. The implementation of sanitary objectives would thus position their city within the ranks of the "civilized." A global competition ensued, an earlier version of the contemporary quest for "world city" status (currently defined through cultural amenities and financial capital), in which cities promoted their sanitary achievements and won sanitary credit on the world stage. In this way, they might distinguish themselves from other cities whose environments remained unruly and their people uncivilized. The flip side of this boosterism coin was the chronic fear that their city's sanitary credit would tumble in the eye of others. For example, Mexico City elites regularly touted at World's Fairs their sanitary achievements to eliminate the miasma-generating floodwaters while at the same time lamenting among themselves that their city resembled disease-ridden urban Africa more than Paris or London. Likewise, Manhattan boosters grew concerned that poor migrants keeping hogs and chicken would dismay European visitors and perpetuate representations of

New York as a filthy place. And, colonial administrators of Singapore feared that without better sanitary protections their city would remain in disrepute as among the most unhealthy in the British Empire (Tenorio Trillo 1996; McNeur 2014; Yeoh 2013; Vitz 2018). Inter-city competition further cemented the global character of the urban-environmental imaginary, understood as sanitation to which all cities needed to aspire.

Drying and Draining: Aquatic Urban Environments in the Age of Sanitation

In the Western imaginary, cities and water have long been held in tension, which the age of sanitation exacerbated. On the one hand, almost all major cities in North America and Europe in the nineteenth century were located on a river, a bay, a lake, a harbor, or an estuary. Likewise, imperial urban hubs were also generally located on such bodies of water. This had everything to do with facilitating the movement of goods and people, including armies and navies, across nations and empires and with guaranteeing ample supplies of foodstuffs. Water quite literally nourished civilization and kept it afloat. On the other hand, too much water – that is, water covering land on which it did not belong (a flood), or, in some instances too little water for navigation, were seen as existential hazards, threats to the proper order of things. Water was lifeblood, but only when properly channeled, controlled, and harnessed to foster specific national communities and imperial projects. Although non-Western peoples also located their cities around water, for the same reasons mentioned earlier, and maintained highly engineered waterscapes, these cultures made fewer distinctions between good and bad water. The term "flood" may have existed in their lexicon, but these cultures also developed agroecological practices that operated within the bounds of fluid ecosystems, places where wet and dry land were rarely fixed (Morris 2012; Candiani 2014; Bhattacharyya 2018; Vann 2021; Hossain 2021). The European quest to "conquer water" stemmed from capitalist agriculture, the development of hydraulic engineering, and state-building endeavors (Merchant 1989; Cronon 1983; Scott 1999; Blackbourn 2006). For example, in Prussia and then unified Germany, engineers drained swamps for commercial agricultural purposes and constructed dikes and dams along the Rhine to prevent flooding, normalize shipping channels, and provide hydropower. Their work over the course of a century made the Rhine watershed among the most industrial areas of the world (Cioc 2002; Blackbourn 2006).

Western hydraulic engineering and water governance, however, were also formed in colonial encounters. For instance, developers and colonial officials hashed out some of the first British legal definitions of fixed, immovable property in early colonial Calcutta on the fluvial Ganga delta, an aquatic space that Native peoples had conceptualized in radically different terms (Bhattacharyya 2018). As Europeans and Euro-descendent peoples expanded their influence into urbanizing coastal and riparian areas during the nineteenth century and as elite imaginaries increasingly emphasized the perils of uncontrolled and stagnant water, more of the world's urban aquatic environments came under greater scrutiny.

Sanitary engineers despised stagnant and unruly water wherever they found it, but they held the aquatic environments in tropical and subtropical colonial cities, as well as the economic, social, and religious practices ensconced within those environments, in special contempt. In these spaces, colonial powers premised racial hierarchies in part on a people's capacity to properly control waterways according to a strict binary of "wet" and "dry." The early development of New Orleans, located on one of the largest wetlands in the world – the Mississippi River delta – required the elimination of Native farming and fishing practices, which both Spanish and French colonizers deemed barbaric. Where Natives saw a rich aquatic environment constantly regenerated by the ebb and flow of the river, Europeans saw natural unpredictability and social poverty, a wasteland that could only be improved through flood control, dryland farming, and clearly demarcated shipping lanes. The French official Bienville sited New Orleans along one such shipping channel, but repressing the water's advance proved futile. Eighteenth- and nineteenth-century New Orleans experienced recurring floods and drainage problems. Rather than a healthy, bustling port city, the French built a rain-soaked and diseased environment, culminating in the yellow fever outbreak of 1853 in which up to 11,000 residents perished (Kelman 2003; Morris 2012). In a great irony of the era of sanitation, urban authorities sometimes worsened the same problems they were trying to resolve in the first place.

On the other side of the world, European imperialists had somewhat better fortune in their quest to transform aquatic environments, if not necessarily in preventing disease outbreaks. The British military doctor James Ranald Martin and other colonial officials also saw the aquatic Ganga delta of changing tides and fluid alluvial sediments (char) as a "wasteland" from which pestilent miasma emanated – a place where "'one would breathe thickly through the heat'" (Bhattacharyya 2018: 19). Official characterizations of the tropical aquatic environment as an inferior moral geography, Debjani Bhattacharyya asserts, helped legitimize the British East India Company's and, later, Raj authorities' endeavors to drain, fill, and reclaim aquatic spaces and fix private property to foster capital accumulation. These endeavors were contested, advancing in fits and starts. Officials sought to substitute the "social value [of land] . . . as a possession involving a complex system of patronage, gifting practices, ancestral spirits and gods" for a regime of fixed, monetized, and inalienable property (Bhattacharyya 2018: 10). Michael Vann traces a similar environmental practice in Hanoi, which the French viewed with disdain – an aquatic space unhealthy, filthy, and inscrutable to a Western rationality that stressed clear property markers and governable subjects. To construct a "modern" city based on Paris, authorities drained the coastal wetlands, reclaimed land from the Red River, and covered the canals upon which local merchants and agriculturalists plied their trade (Logan 2000; Vann 2021). Similarly, to the south in the Mekong Delta, private contractors built canals by dredging muddy delta waters to connect sugar and rice plantations to markets in bustling Saigon and beyond (Biggs 2010).

The Americans' construction of the Panama Canal, among the most celebrated examples of Western hydraulic engineering, similarly foreclosed other aquatic imaginaries and practices. American engineers and public health officials eradicated the vibrant water-borne economies of the lowland Isthmus, peppered with towns and small cities that were already integrated into a global market economy, and replaced them with the imperially controlled and highly re-engineered landscape. The new canal meandered around a number of urban settlements that US authorities built in ways that segregated American managers from ethnically diverse workers (Lasso 2019). In all these instances fluid and aquatic ecologies, and the social relations that sustained them, contradicted the colonial impetus behind the global urban-environmental imaginary – and thus had to be extirpated.

These urban-environmental transformations, however, were not representative of a predetermined modernization where the traditional, fluid, and communal uniformly gave way to the liberal, fixed, and modern. Bhattacharyya (2018) underscores simultaneous and overlapping experiences, not clearly defined temporal differences between pre- and post-colonial arrangements. The aquatic nature of the delta at Calcutta rarely obeyed the commands of engineers and landowners, and landscapes often remained "fugitive" over long periods of time. Moreover, colonial bureaucrats were compelled to accommodate river spirits and Hindu deities within the colonial legal proceedings over land tenure. Similarly, historian Brodwyn Fischer explains how the aquatic landscape of Recife on the Atlantic coast of Brazil, settled and built by recently emancipated Afro-Brazilians, did not fit its boosters' modernizing script of formalized social relations, settlement on fixed and dried land, and service provision. Fischer traces the experiences of Afro-Brazilians in an urban environment simultaneously made and silenced by liberal modernity. The informal patronage relations of Afro-Brazilian communities in Recife, tied to hinterland sugar plantations, were integral to Recife's experience as, in the words of Jennifer Robinson, an "ordinary city" of global modernity (Robinson 2006; Fischer 2022). Fischer warns against urban historians replicating the teleological scripts of cities converging into a uniform modernity. Global urban historians must trace the spatial convergences and temporal ruptures brought on by the world's structural integration, to be sure, but must also be cognizant of the formative power of vernacular social relations and landscapes and how those vernacular conditions intertwine with modernizing impulses.

Sanitary Infrastructure, Urban Environmental Governance, and Racialization

Chadwickian sanitation planners often analogized the city to an organism whose circulatory flows must be properly maintained in order to optimize its health. Only through healthy circulation – of water and air – would deadly miasmas be kept in check. Sanitarians went to work starting in the 1840s to bring sanitary infrastructure – combined water and sewerage as well as green spaces – to major urban areas throughout not only Europe and the United States but also independent Latin America and Europe's numerous colonial possessions. The bibliography on the history of urban sanitary infrastructure is long, but most are limited spatially to the city, the nation, or the empire (Tarr 1996; Melosi 2000; Prashad 2001;Troesken 2004; McFarlane 2008). A select few venture into trans-imperial or metropolitan North Atlantic comparisons, but we know little about the global history of urban sanitary services – a history of expertise, changing urban ecologies, and the socioenvironmental inequalities made by these infrastructures and services (Rodgers 1998; Platt 2005; Hungerford and Smiley 2016). It is beyond the scope of this synthetic interpretation to address all three of these topics in more than a cursory way. What existing scholarship does permit is an examination of the ways the construction, maintenance, and extension of sanitary infrastructure intersected with regimes of governance – liberal republican and colonial – real estate capital, and processes of racialization across global landscapes. In tracing these relationships, we get a clearer understanding of how urban authorities represented distinct urban environments, how urban populations engaged with these representations, and the reasons why some people received sanitary services and others did not. In this part, I argue that the extension and durability of these large technical systems were determined by the intersections of class power, popular participation, and racist hierarchies within different state structures. In effect, the politics of sanitation, in which countervailing currents of universalism and exclusion coexisted, made and remade urban ecologies in diverse ways across the globe.

In metropolitan and republican national contexts, experts – from doctors to engineers – rhetorically framed their sanitation task with the principle of universality: for a city to have health-giving flow, every resident must be able to access clean water and properly dispose of their wastes. The call for universally extended services coincided with liberal notions, honored more in the breach, of popular sovereignty and citizenship. The transatlantic Progressive era of urban reform during the first two decades of the twentieth century reinforced these principles. Bourgeois reformers, including middle-class women, denounced the iniquitous practices of private service contractors and industrialists whose pursuit of profit deteriorated health conditions in the home, on the street, and in the workplace. Some also denounced landlords who refused to maintain adequate housing in working-class districts. The reformers Jane Addams, Florence Kelley, Mary McDowell, and Alice Hamilton of the settlement movement in Chicago were among the most outspoken and organized of this middle-class urban-environmental Progressivism, but they were more exemplary of a wider transatlantic reform movement than extraordinary figures. The reforms of this era reinforced state and technocratic authority and an urban episteme of order, cleanliness, and environmental control while addressing ongoing urban sanitary inequities spawned by rapid industrialization (Platt 2005; Estabrook, Levenstein, and Wooding 2018; Boughton 2018; Browning 2022).

The more radical of these urban Progressives built alliances with labor groups and socialists in a period when "progressivism" and "socialism" were often used interchangeably. Labor and socialist groups, who were expanding definitions of citizenship across Europe and the Americas, demanded sanitary housing and service installment in working-class neighborhoods. The "sewer socialists" (or less pejoratively "constructive socialists") of Milwaukee came to power in 1910, an outlier in terms of Progressives' achievement of sustained municipal power but also broadly representative of environmentally informed working-class politics in industrializing cities across liberal republican spaces (Booth 1985; Meade 1989; Baer 1998; Dogliani 2002; Estabrook et al. 2018; Vitz 2018; Rector 2022; Fogelson 2022; Haderer 2023). Notions of citizenship and accountable government animated, in some instances, non-white and multiracial working class politics for adequate and sanitary housing, as Natalia Molina (2006) has demonstrated in her study of Mexican-American struggles for improved housing conditions during the Great Depression. Even in Mexico, under modernizing dictator Porfirio Díaz, and in Restorationist Spain, working-class residents of Mexico City, Morelia, Madrid, and elsewhere beseeched municipal governments to extend sanitary infrastructure to their neighborhoods and homes. They employed the language of sanitation and liberal citizenship, boasting of their propriety as citizens deserving of modern services, and offered their own labor and monetary resources to build the infrastructure themselves (Jiménez 2019; Vorms 2022).

Much of the landmark literature in North American and European urban environmental history explicitly state or implicitly suggests that water and sewer networks between the 1840s and about 1920 were universally extended in most urban areas. Officials moved to municipalize many private utilities such as water, guaranteeing the networked city as an urban right. However, urban class power constrained the quality of those services once they entered the domestic sphere. It was one thing to challenge private utilities and invest in urban infrastructure for economic production and public health; it was quite another for political elites to challenge urban developers and meddle with the property rights of urban landowners. Herein lay the limits of Progressive reformers, such as Chicago's settlement leaders, who struggled to ensure adequate sewerage and water connection inside tenements and apartments and waste disposal in neighborhoods (Platt 2005; Washington 2005; Bernhardt 2011). In many Latin American cities and throughout much of urban Mediterranean Europe where informal peripheral settlements comprised of recent rural migrants sprang up at the same time municipalities installed sanitary infrastructure, service extensions often stopped at the boundaries of the "legal" city, thus helping to produce the idea of the "slum" as a problem of social and hygienic marginalization (Fischer 2014; Vorms 2022; Bartolini 2023). This, combined with, in general, more cash-strapped state and municipal budgets helped cause the ongoing disparities in sanitary service provision between North Atlantic cities, on the one hand, and Latin American and many European Mediterranean cities on the other, despite shared republican political traditions and similarly vibrant urban working-class political practices. Similarly, in early Soviet Moscow undergoing rapid industrialization, hundreds of thousands of rural migrants arrived to settlements outside the formal city of Soviet institutions bereft of public services and adequate housing (Hoffman 1994).

Too many urban historians elide the complex and dynamic relationships between race and racism, on the one hand, and sanitary infrastructure on the other. To be sure, many sanitarians, such as the renowned Osbert Chadwick who worked for a time in colonial Hong Kong, did not overtly organize their theories around race (Downs 2021). They strove for universal services as the best weapon against disease – whether disease was understood through miasma and environment or micro-organisms. Harold Platt (2006), moreover, suggests that overt racist understandings of insanitation during the nineteenth century – directed against the putatively innate attributes of Jews and European immigrant populations – gave way to a class-based moral reformism during the Progressive era. Yet, as numerous historians have asserted, racialization was inextricably tied to the sanitary paradigm from the outset. Indeed, the science of public health helped produce modern racial hierarchies (Molina 2006).

Thinking at a global scale, racist hierarchies were a key determinant of why some urban residents enjoyed adequate water, sewerage, and other services while others did not. Several historians of the US South and booming cities in the North have assumed that basic sanitary services did not extend to black neighborhoods (Tomes 1998; Russell 1982). However, Werner Troesken, in *Water, Race, and Disease* (2004), revises this narrative by seeking to resolve an apparent paradox of African-American history: Why did black mortality rates decline throughout the US South between 1900 and 1940, at the peak of Jim Crow segregation when blacks' access to medical services were limited and wages stagnant? He argues that municipalities did, in fact, extend water and sewer infrastructure, with only a few exceptions, throughout the urban South curtailing water-borne diseases like typhoid, diarrhea, and cholera. In an ironic twist, he argues that it was precisely because of racism that cities extended sanitary networks to black residents. At a time when residential neighborhood-level segregation in the South was incipient, whites, living in close proximity to blacks, invested in cleaning up and installing sanitary infrastructure in their streets and neighborhoods, actions that coincidentally benefitted blacks as well. Troesken explains (xv): "To die from typhoid was one thing. To die from typhoid caught by drinking water tainted with the wastes of a black man's privy was quite another."

This provocative argument does not tell the whole story about the relationship between race and sanitary service provision across a diverse US urban landscape. In fact, one historian has questioned Troesken's claims that inequalities between urban black and white mortality rates declined during this period and that water and sewer provision accounted for rising black life expectancy in the US South (Harper 2007). Moving beyond this specific debate, in the second half of the nineteenth century, US-American Protestant elites generally viewed non-Protestant working-class immigrants from Eastern Europe, Southern Europe, and Ireland as ethnically and culturally inferior and therefore not fully white. For example, in cities like Chicago and Detroit, Eastern European immigrants faced horrific sanitary conditions, and their neighborhoods either lacked most sanitary services altogether or were priced out of the market for clean water (Washington 2005; Rector 2022).

As black migrants from the South settled in these and other newer segregated neighborhoods and as ethnic whites moved out (in the process claiming whiteness by means of anti-blackness), the black working class faced the burden of urban-environmental injustice (Washington 2005; Rector 2022). In Memphis, the segregated black population was excluded entirely from the sewer system. Other non-white populations also faced similarly deplorable conditions. Los Angeles' Chinese community was deemed unreformable by local public health authorities and thus excluded from that city's sewer network (Duffy 1990; Molina 2006). Although more research is needed, the role of race in the provision of key sanitary services in the late nineteenth- and early twentieth-century United States has much to do with the degree of residential racial segregation in cities at the time comprehensive hydraulic infrastructure was built. Landlords' efforts to skirt building codes also intersected with racial segregation to concentrate unsanitary housing conditions – broken sewer lines, incomplete bathrooms, communal taps in tenements, reliance on neighborhood wells, and inconsistent water pressure – in black and brown communities.

In colonial spaces, the "rule of colonial difference" – Partha Chatterjee's term to explain colonial subjugation in an era of supposed liberal universality – applied (1993: 17–18). There, race was often an even more conspicuous variable in sanitary service provision. Two interacting ideological premises undergirded modern colonialism: the civilizing impulse that purported a future universal improvement despite difference, on the one hand, and exclusion and separation whereby the colonized were deemed inherently backward, on the other. On the surface, sanitarians reinforced the civilizing impulse – European experts would civilize the colonized and prepare them for self-governance in a similar way as they were civilizing their own lower classes back home (Zeheter 2015). Yet, while there were certainly examples of colonial sanitarians who embraced this civilizing impulse to bring public health to all and uplift colonial subjects, most top colonial officials at the end of the nineteenth century generally doubted their subjects' capacity of civilization, at least in the short term. Hygienic improvement and a group's capacity to achieve civilization fit like hand in glove. The unclean, wasteful, and inferior Native who could not comprehend the progress represented by new sanitary services starkly contrasted with the idealized European, rational and clean, who either knew how to progress or could be instructed to do so – even as full citizenship rights were withheld from many working-class European and US-American populations. Native resistance to European closure of their alternative water sources and the specific cultural uses of that water, meanwhile, served to reinforce the colonial racial hierarchy (Arnold 1993; Gandy 2008). Ultimately, the reach of sanitary service infrastructure hinged on the interplay between liberal universalism and the rule of colonial difference, different colonial regimes, and the environmental conditions of the overseas tropics.

The rule of colonial difference intermingled with urban class relations in ways that sometimes produced unexpected constellations of colonial power. In late nineteenth-century Hong Kong, British authorities condemned the Chinese-owned tenements for violating "every rule of sanitation in regard to drainage, ventilation, and cleanliness" and called for more stringent building codes, better ventilated living spaces, and sanitary service extensions. But laissez-faire urbanization, spawned by the fear that regulations would scare investors and drive down property revenue, in combination with Chinese property owners' seemingly paradoxical invocation of colonial difference hindered reformers' attempts. While many doctors and engineers believed the Chinese Natives could become more hygienic once afforded a more positive environment, Chinese property owners advanced a racialized environmental conception more typically associated with colonial rule. In a petition to authorities against a proposal to revamp Chinese housing along sanitary lines, Chinese landlords argued that Chinese people were long accustomed to "'living in large and crowded cities' ... and would not understand the reason [and] would in no way avail themselves of the facilities for the free access of light and air" (Chu 2013: 24; Chu 2022). These Chinese elites posited essential racial difference – that the mass of Chinese poor were culturally incompatible with European notions of sanitation and living standards. They claimed that any alterations along European lines would be counterproductive in practice, leading to alleyways being used as "'receptacles for the deposit of refuse and filth'" (Chu 2013: 24).

When the topic turned to water supply, however, the same Chinese property owners changed their tune, siding with sanitarians such as Osbert Chadwick who called for a universal water supply network (Chu 2013: 27–28). Facing a wave of expert advice to extend water service, colonial officials had connected hundreds of tenements to the water system, but when a long drought that beset the region in the late 1890s caused shortages in European homes, the state's calculus changed. Officials brandished the weapon of colonial difference to legitimize a legislative proposal to stop services to Chinese tenements and other residences. This time the Chinese property owners, invoking the trope of liberal universalism and the concerns of tropical medicine, argued that if an adequate supply of water is considered essential in the temperate climate of England, "'should not a constant supply of water be considered an absolute necessity for every tenement house in a tropical climate like Hong Kong?'" (Chu 2013: 29). Eventually, the Chinese elites got their water service restored (Carroll 2005). These cases illustrate the different ways that material class power over land and racial hierarchies intersected to produce colonial environmental governance in one urban setting.

The different experiences of Quebec, a settler colonial city, and Madras in British India serve to further illustrate the ways colonial racism intersected with the urban-environmental imaginary. Whereas during the middle of the nineteenth century Quebec's government built an integrated water and drainage system that serviced a vast majority of the white settler population, Madras' colonial government funded and completed theirs much later, and only when British interests were at stake. Early government officials and engineers in India, including Madras, took a conservative position that generally rejected engagement with the colonized. "In their view," Michael Zeheter maintains (2015: 156), "sanitation was for Europe and not for India. If a colonial city like Quebec funded a waterworks ... because it aspired to European levels of civilization, that was Quebec's business. The moral arguments for improvements there did not apply to Madras." The diseases that ravaged the British army in the Crimean war, the 1857 Sepoy (Indian soldiers under British authority) rebellion, and a major cholera outbreak originating in Egypt in 1865 altered colonial officials' position. At that point, reformers authorized Madras' water supply system. Still, the system primarily serviced the British military barracks, understood as "'islands of purity in the miasmatic landscape'" (Suhit Guha in McFarlane 2008). Meanwhile, a planned sewer system did not receive any funding (Zeheter 2015).

British-controlled Singapore's Native residents received similar treatment. The colonial government provided latrines rather than installing a more expensive sewer system given that, officials believed, Asians possessed unsanitary habits indicative of the "failure of their civilization" (Yeoh 2013: 205). In many Asian cities under British rule, colonial powerholders' anxieties over popular protest and the legitimacy of their power also mitigated the building and extension of sanitary infrastructure. British officials feared the organized power of night soil workers and water carriers in China's treaty port cities and in Singapore at the same time that European residents would have much preferred to gain their independence from such workers, who were thought to be backward and dirty (Rogaski 2004; Stapleton 2022). Sanitary infrastructures and services physically segregated urban spaces and reinforced colonial hierarchies across British colonial cities.

This is more than just a story about the British Empire. Just as sanitary infrastructure and the urban segregation it produced varied within imperial spaces, they varied equally, if not more, trans-imperially. Different colonial budgeting schemes influenced the installment and governance of sanitary infrastructure. Whereas the British rejected financing major urban infrastructural projects in their African colonies and elsewhere due to restrictive colonial budgeting policies, the French at least purported budgetary equality, causing slight variations in service provision, and thus arguably, access to a healthy environment (Hungerford and Smiley 2016). The Dutch, however, wholeheartedly rejected funding the civilizing impulse in Batavia (now Jakarta, Indonesia), and favored a racial regime of absolute inequality and colonial inferiority (Kooy and Bakker 2008; Stapleton 2022). And, the Spanish cared little for urban sanitary improvement in the Philippines, an omission that served as one of the many justifications of US military intervention there in 1898 (Stapleton 2022).

Following the 1842 Treaty of Nanjing between Britain and Qing China, dozens of China's coastal and riverine cities were opened to foreign "concessions" – the so-called treaty port cities. These port cities – such as Guangzhou and Tianjin – became sites of inter-imperial rivalry as each foreign government aimed to showcase its own brand of "hygienic modernity:" the regulation of water flows in and out of residences and concession neighborhoods. In Tianjin, the ability of concession elites to showcase their hygienic modernity was determined by each concession's geographic location – the Japanese, in particular, were inconvenienced by low-lying swampy lands – and their financial flexibility (Rogaski 2004). Yet despite these important variations, most European residents, and a minority of wealthy Natives, received private taps with running water and sewer hook-ups whereas the colonized generally had to share communal taps and visit standpipes with inconsistent flow and, in some cases, high fees (Kooy and Bakker 2008; McFarlane 2008; Hungerford and Smiley 2016).

The political and economic centrality of particular colonial cities also helped determine the extent of service provision. In general, colonial governments prioritized so-called hard (or "economic") infrastructure over soft (or "social") infrastructure, so railroads, ports, and other projects considered essential for commerce received the bulk of the funding over sanitation projects (Straeten 2016). Therefore, only where capital investments were concentrated and political control imperative was soft infrastructure more likely to also be prioritized. As a political and commercial center, Calcutta installed water service earlier than other major British colonial urban centers, and the building of New Delhi in the 1910s to serve as the new Raj capital required major investments in sanitation (Hosagrahar 2005; Mann 2007; Legg 2013).

Colonial officials' refusal to adapt their blueprints made for the European metropole to local, and often mysterious, environmental and climatic conditions also shaped infrastructural provision and efficacy. Bombay's chief engineer Henry Coynbeare imported gravitational water supply schemes that had worked so effectively in places like Glasgow and Liverpool (Broich 2007). However, when confronted with tropical humidity, high heat, heavy rainfall, soil conditions, and seismic activity, these systems faced long construction delays and, once completed, could deteriorate quickly or even break down entirely. Bombay's workers buried pipes underground, just as had been done in Britain to avoid freezing temperatures, but the long iron-made mainline began to rust after a few decades because engineers were unaware of the salinity of the soil. Similarly, Bombay's reservoir, built with Britain's climate in mind, was quickly overtaken by algae from the tropical sun, impoverishing the quality of the water (Broich 2007). Similar inadequacies and environmental obstacles dogged other colonial sanitary infrastructure in Singapore and Hong Kong. More research is needed outside British possessions, but, in general, European colonizers were quick to point out the racial and epidemiological threats the tropical climate posed to Europeans, but when it came to infrastructural development, the technological hubris to conquer nature prevailed.

Unlike in many liberal republican cities where notions of political equality, national belonging and worthiness, public health discourse, and accountable (if often cash-strapped) government animated working-class politics around sanitation stretching from Europe to the Americas, colonial settings produced different urban-environmental politics. Actual colonial investments in sanitary services like water, sewerage, and waste removal rarely matched the prominence of colonial discourses about "civilizing" natives through Western medicine and public health interventions. Instead, health interventions tended to be more coercive in the colonies, involving surveillance, intrusions into private settings, forced vaccination campaigns, and the like. Unsurprisingly, many Indigenous populations, who held different beliefs about health and disease, resisted. Nonetheless, the discourses of Western public health and sanitation became dominant over time insofar as educated Native elites had to engage with them in one way or another, whether through outright rejection in favor of non-Western paradigms, or through accommodation and appropriation to advance nationalist causes (Arnold 1993; Ghosh 2022). With regard to sanitary services specifically, Indigenous elites in colonial Jakarta and the Chinese landlords of Hong Kong accepted colonial water infrastructures but excoriated the inequalities inherent in their deployment. The ostensibly public system in Jakarta, for example, provided free private connections to Europeans but public taps for the Native population who were obligated to pay a fee. In highlighting the iniquitous water system in their critique of colonial rule, Native elites threatened "to disrupt the colonial system of classification" wherein colonists embraced technical infrastructures and the colonized devalued them (Kooy and Bakker 2008: 382). In Japanese-occupied Seoul, colonial officials effected a similar set of sanitary interventions as their Western counterparts did elsewhere, treating Native Koreans as culturally inferior, unclean, and lacking in "civic morality" but ultimately assimilable to Japan's hygienic modernity. Many Koreans resisted forced vaccinations and mandatory cleanup campaigns, and the educated elite adopted a nationalist stance that chastised Japanese officials for prioritizing policing and punishment over investments in adequate housing and sanitary infrastructure (Henry 2014). In this way, colonized elites, from Hong Kong and Jakarta to Seoul, appropriated the urban-environmental imaginary. They called for more robust investments in sanitary infrastructure and the education of poor Natives, who they maintained lacked proper hygienic customs. Our understanding of the global history of sanitary infrastructure remains incomplete. We require more comparative and global studies, as well as more case studies of particular cities and regions, to complete this preliminary, if suggestive, analysis that explores class conflict, racialization, environmental dynamics, and liberal and colonial forms of statecraft.

The Urban Ecology of Segregation and the Policing of Public Health

Governments' efforts to build sanitary infrastructure not only symbolically distinguished the civilized from the uncivilized but also, in many cities, materially reinforced racial segregation. In fact, such practices of residential segregation, and the policing of hygiene practices more generally, operated through a racialized understanding of disease ecologies. Although racist understandings of salubriousness and disease were not the sole ideological drivers of residential segregation, the two phenomena are impossible to disentangle (Curtin 1985; Njoh 2012). It is this intertwined history of segregation and urban representations of disease, and their global intellectual and biological interconnections, to which I now turn.

Carl Nightingale (2012) explains the ways "city splitters" (doctors, developers, engineers, planners, and colonial officials) of the nineteenth and early twentieth centuries conceived racial segregation as an environmental project of urban transformation. According to Nightingale, the environmental theory of disease complemented, in some ways, modern racialization. Races had their own homelands, the theory went, and while tropical natives might be susceptible to disease, they were more innately amenable to tropical climate. Whites, on the other hand, more easily succumbed to heat, humidity, and disease. Moreover, miasmas were more likely to beset the humid tropics, especially aquatic tropical cities like Calcutta, than northern climes. Although some Europeans believed that white settlement in the tropics was unviable, there also developed a strong streak of thought that emphasized environmental interventions to make urban tropical lands habitable.

The biological and intellectual connections between London and Calcutta fostered the first comprehensive plans for residential segregation, based on this environmental theory of disease and race. London and its modest early sanitary reforms, for many British colonialists, heralded a similar colonial transformation, and Governor General Richard Wellesley introduced new governing mechanisms in Calcutta that in some ways surpassed London's transformations.

The main objective was to forge a place "'where Englishmen, having the usual constitution of their race, can live in the full possession of their faculties, and their vigor.'" Officials commenced street-widening projects to facilitate the movement of air and clear miasmas understood to carry malaria and, by 1817, cholera. In contrast, Natives, living in dense quarters, were perceived to carry such diseases threaten the health of whites (Nightingale 2012: 92).

In the decades that followed, upon the arrival of cholera to England, which was seen as an unwelcome import from Calcutta's miasmatic environment, city officials built the colony's first comprehensive water supply and sewer systems to service "white town" – the name given to the British encampment in contradistinction to "black town" – and drain waste from the pestilent Hooghly river. British developers modeled the slightly more elevated "white town" on London's elite West End. They built similar Palladian villas but also erected high walls to enclose their compounds. The private compounds, street widening, the higher elevation, water supply, and gravity-induced drainage combined to curtail, or so they thought, Native disease and insalubrity (Nightingale 2012). The racial segregation of Calcutta through sanitary reform and real estate development proved incomplete. Regardless, more coercive and determined city splitters elsewhere in the colonial world borrowed heavily from the schemes of Calcutta's elites, and the fear of diseased colonial spaces continued to shape racial segregation.

The British military stations, or cantonments, had the purpose of ruling over vast territories of South Asia, but their design had implications beyond pure military domination. The cantonments (also called hill stations because of their high altitude and thus distance from Indigenous towns) constituted another attempt to accomplish what Calcutta segregationists struggled to do: enclose the race of the conquerors within refuges of fresh air, vegetation, and less stultifying heat and humidity, away from the pestilent miasmas and filthy Native towns ridden with malaria (Nightingale 2012; Ghosh 2022). The British transported their hill stations to their new African possessions. Similarly, the French designed resort spa towns in colonies from Tunisia and Madagascar to Guadeloupe to cure colonists of tropical maladies and separate the races. Authorities in French Dakar went further: they designed a "hygienic village" for Europeans, an elevated town on a plateau separated from the Native population in which no traditional African structure was permitted (Jennings 2006; Njoh 2012).

The intersections of racism and disease that contributed to global segregation practice hardened at the turn of the century with the bacteriological revolution and Social Darwinism. The pendulum of colonial rule swung further away from liberal universalism and toward theories of innate racial inferiority wherein colonized peoples were deemed more inherently prone to disease because of fixed unhygienic morals and behaviors. As many scholars have maintained, this hardened racist understanding of urban health complemented many colonial elites' desires to distance themselves from natives and police and raze infected spaces, rather than invest in universal infrastructural development under the banner of amelioration (Nightingale 2012; Yeoh 2013). City splitting and racialized public health surveillance fit like hand in glove. The third bubonic plague pandemic underscored this altered environmental imaginary and fostered a new wave of segregation and exclusionary urban governance.

The bubonic plague, which had been circulating among wild rodents in the Himalayas, made its way to the major colonial port city of Hong Kong from Canton province in 1894. From there, the bacteria spread to Bombay, a key node in the British cotton trade, and then across Africa and the Pacific world at the turn of the century. As the plague besieged colonial cities, authorities strengthened racialized theories of disease and executed a combination of invasive environmental measures and cordon sanitaires. Many of these measures, and their sanitary reforms more generally, likely worsened the outbreak of the plague in urban centers. Historian Michael Vann argues that the construction of Hanoi's sewer system created an ecological home for Norway rats that preferred underground spaces and often transmitted plague-carrying flees to the black rats that inhabited buildings and alleyways (Vann and Clarke 2019). Officials' cleaning campaigns often included clearing sewer systems; Bombay city officials, for example, in a desperate attempt to curb the disease, injected three million gallons of carbolic acid and saltwater daily into the city's sewers and drains, likely forcing plague-carrying rats into encounters with people in homes and streets (Echenberg 2007; Nightingale 2012). Moreover, quarantine ships often docked in port after the last human plague case, sending plague-carrying flees on shore and back into poor neighborhoods adjacent to the ports (Nightingale 2012).

"Segregation mania," as Nightingale calls it, followed the plague, racializing urban danger and insalubrity wherever it spread. Dr. James A Lowson, who headed the segregationist and coercive anti-plague campaign in both Hong Kong and Bombay, mandated that thousands of people presumed to inhabit plague hotspots, the poor and working-class areas of the respective cities, be moved to "isolation hospitals" – to the designated and infamous hospital boat *Hygeia* in the case of Hong Kong – and segregation camps elsewhere. And, officials seized properties and destroyed hundreds of residences (Echenberg 2007; Nightingale 2012: 166–167) (see Figure 1). Bombay officials established the Bombay Improvement Company that sought to restore the city's "sanitary credit" by issuing new building codes and resettling thousands of Natives on the outskirts of town (Chhabria 2019). The British

Figure 1 Destruction of housing in the Tai Ping Shan area, Hong Kong, 1895.
Courtesy of Soldiers of Shropshire Museum

established other urban Improvement Companies, all with similar objectives
across their possessions at the time of the plague. Historian Sheetal Chhabria
locates the origins of the modern slum in these anti-plague campaigns, and calls
its physical and symbolic creation "a case of a solution finding its problem
rather than the other way around" (Chhabria 2019: 181). Upon the plague's
arrival in Honolulu in 1900, American officials viewed Chinatown as an immi-
nent danger to the health of white American residents. They debated Bombay
and Hong Kong's plague responses, settling on what Hong Kong authorities had
ultimately rejected: fire. Winds swept through the city during one controlled
burn, torching all of Chinatown. Residents were then forced into plague camps
outside the city and kept under armed guard for months. The following year,
upon the mere hint of plague entering San Francisco, police forbade movement
to and from Chinatown while the city's press stoked fears of plague-carrying
Chinese wandering the city (Shah 2001; Echenberg 2007; Nightingale 2012).

Racialized peoples negotiated these isolationist and segregationist policies in
diverse ways. Some fled to the hinterlands, while others stayed put and concealed
sick peoples from official surveillance and did not cooperate with health authorities. Chinese residents, for example, were able to rebuild in situ Honolulu's
Chinatown, and in Hong Kong colonized subjects' backlash led authorities to lift
the most draconian anti-plague measures (Shah 2001; Yeoh 2013).

Nonetheless, the pandemic fostered racialized conceptions of disease and similar segregation efforts across continents. British colonial health officer Dr. W.J. Simpson, stationed in Nairobi at the height of the city's plague outbreak, admonished in a stunning report that "the diseases 'to which these different races are respectively liable are readily transferable to the European especially 'when their dwellings are near each other.'" He called for "a neutral belt of unoccupied territory at least 300 yards in width" separating European from Asians and Africans across British colonial lands (Nightingale 2012: 181; Odari 2021). And when plague visited the already-segregated French Dakar in 1914, authorities burnt all Native housing around the "hygienic village" to safeguard the health of all European residents and relocated Natives to a new segregated town even farther away. In 1910s and 1920s Leopoldville, now Kinshasa, the capital of the Democratic Republic of Congo, Belgian authorities created a European district separated from the Native town by a cordon sanitaire where a botanical garden, a zoo, and a golf course were sited (Njoh 2012).

Sanitary-based segregation was also motivated by fears of malaria across colonial Africa at the turn of the century. In German-controlled Cameroon, for example, authorities located their capital, Kamerun, on the slopes of Mount Cameroon, to safeguard German administrators from the pestilent low-lying tropics that harbored malaria-carrying mosquitoes (Njoh 2012).

It is also important that we not exaggerate the physical and cultural separation and political powerlessness that segregation intended to create. Intermingling was common as Europeans relied on a Native workforce, and colonial rulers were often more effective at projecting visual and representative power over Indigenous peoples, rooted in racist discourses, and the segregated spaces they inhabited than real political power (Mitchell 1988; Chattopadhyay 2005). In some instances, Native elites had some autonomy to govern themselves. In early twentieth-century Calcutta, Hindu professionals – an assortment of educated elites – adapted the colonialist civilizing discourses of hygiene and mixed it with their religious beliefs. They then applied it to "inferior" Muslim inhabitants, reinforcing caste hierarchies in the city. (Ghosh 2022)

This racialized imaginary of urban maladies reflected the imperatives of colonial capitalism. Public health officials prioritized plague containment to maintain global trade and avoid the humiliation that accompanied status as a plague hotspot – which only revealed the ineffectiveness of a state's power to control people and environment. Only the most progressive of the old sanitarians – Osbert Chadwick for instance – proposed improvements to the neighborhoods inflicted by the disease, and even Chadwick failed to challenge the inequalities inherent in the colonial project itself. Anti-plague measures varied across time and space, and included, in some places such as French Hanoi, a comprehensive rat hunt, but at the core of those measures laid a politics of spatial isolation and segregation: cordoning off, expelling, displacing, and even burning, often with the purpose of claiming prime urban land (Vann and Clarke 2019; Vann 2021). Authorities failed categorically to address any of the social-systemic and infrastructural causes of the pandemic – the global movement of commodities such as cotton and the unequal urban ecosystems that put plague-carrying rats in direct contact with workers in the ports and the residents of nearby neighborhoods.

Conclusion

Over the course of the nineteenth century, urban ecologies, for all their idiosyncrasies of climate, hydrology, and other biophysical elements, became globally integrated in important ways. Commerce across imperial and metro-politan networks brought about similar port infrastructures and working-class populations, both bonded and free, to haul, transport, and process the raw materials of plantation and industrial capitalism in fast-growing cities. These commercial exchanges, despite different levels of industrialization between metropolitan and colonial spaces, made the biological transfer of disease inevitable and created similarly unequal urban ecologies. Colonial commer-cial capitalism, increasingly driven by industrial resource needs in Europe and the United States, helped to spawn a shared urban-environmental imaginary in which state power – whether metropolitan or colonial – was required to regulate flows, sanitize populations, and achieve "civilization." In the nine-teenth and early twentieth centuries, racist structures and class power – of developers and landlords, especially – geographical conditions, as well as popular resistance and incipient anti-colonial nationalisms, shaped global urban-environmental governance.

The rise of urban forestry also illustrates the global form of environmental governance. In the second half of the nineteenth century, scientists and engin-eers shared a belief that trees comprised the pillars of public health by regulating climate and airflow and preventing desiccation. These ideas were articulated by nineteenth-century scientists such as Alexander von Humboldt and then circu-lated among urban professionals in sanitary and town planning conferences at the turn of the century. Similarly, urban parks were viewed as civilizing spaces for healthy and wholesome leisure and excursionist activities. Some of the more progressive urban foresters, like the Olmsted brothers in the United States, France's Jean Claude Forestier, and Mexico's "apostle of the tree," Miguel Ángel de Quevedo, shared a democratic and utilitarian spirit. They sought to provide parks for the urban masses, in part to quell class conflict, although building them generally had the effect of raising property values and creating new urban class inequalities. In colonial contexts, the politics of urban trees were more acutely racialized; parks and gardens served to demarcate the segregated white enclave, sheltered by cover of vegetation from the "diseased" other and the harsh tropical climate (Davis 2007; Mann and Sehrawat 2009; Libertun de Deren 2012; Valenzuela Aguilera 2014; Peckham 2015).

Much of the literature on sanitary infrastructure and urban-environmental governance during the nineteenth and early twentieth centuries either downplays racism and its impacts or treats it as a symptom of colonial difference that does not obtain in metropolitan settings. The former limits our historical understanding of urban-political ecologies. The latter spatially misrepresents the politics of sanitation as a binary between metropolitan universalism and overseas coloniality. What I have tried to show here is the way that racism and the class relations springing from commercial capitalism and landed capital pervaded the sanitary and environmental practices of urban authorities across the globe. What mattered was not whether the particular form of government was "liberal" and rooted in some version of popular sovereignty or "colonial" but, rather, the ways in which racist thinking included and excluded certain people from the body politic. State officials' and other elites' disgust for the poor's supposed lack of hygiene and self-care was widespread across the United States and Europe in the nineteenth century, but ultimately they came to view working-class whites, including immigrant nationalities assimilable to whiteness and bourgeois norms, as worthy of proper sanitation. But such status rarely applied, or applied unevenly, to racialized populations, even in the United States and Brazil, both under liberal republicanism. Their urban experiences had much in common with colonial practices, where racial hierarchies and urban class power intersected to determine environmental interventions, as well as the possibilities of popular politics to redress environmental inequalities. Both this universalism and its racist exclusionary counterpart, alike, served hegemonic political functions. On the one hand, ruling elites needed to obfuscate the highly exploitative class relations within bourgeoning industrial capitalism by providing public services. On the other hand, they were incentivized to divide working-class people along racial lines to curb class solidarities.

Urban-environmental governance was a double-edged sword that, on one side, was coercive and punitive and generally racialized, but on the other, created new subjectivities that could turn against existing power structures. It is this other side, which I have alluded to already, that I want to explore further here. In California, Chinese middle-class immigrants articulated a counternarrative to the predominant one of racialized exclusion based on hygiene to support their being extended the same health and sanitary services guaranteed to white citizens (Shah 2001).

Concurrently, in colonial Batavia (now Jakarta), anti-colonial critics called out the water supply system that did not reach Native communities (kampongs) and where the system did arrive, residents were charged a usage fee (Kooy and Bakker 2008). Similarly, in Calcutta, Native peoples embraced their sanitary citizenship to highlight the wrongs of the colonial order (Pande 2010). Meanwhile, the anti-plague response by colonial and sovereign governments generated widespread resistance, from British India, where Walter Rand, head of the Bombay anti-plague committee, was assassinated, to South Africa and urban Brazil, where anti-colonial and national-popular movements centered claims to urban land, autonomy, and health (Chalhoub 1996; Echenberg 2007; Meade 1998). The urban-environmental component of anti-colonialism was pointedly captured by the Martinican Marxist psychiatrist Frantz Fanon (2004: 4):

> The colonist's sector is a sector built to last, all stone and steel. It's a sector of lights and paved roads .... . The colonist's feet can never be glimpsed ... protected by solid shoes in a sector where the streets are clean and smooth .... The colonized's sector ... is a disreputable place inhabited by disreputable people .... .It's a world with no space, people are piled one on top of the other, the shacks squeezed tightly together. The colonized's sector is a famished sector, hungry for bread, meat, shoes, coal, and light.

The remarkable impact of the global-environmental imaginary espoused by doctors, engineers, and health officials bent on urban sanitation was not that it successfully eradicated disease or conquered "nature" but, rather, that it simultaneously strengthened racist urban governance *and* produced widespread agreement among popular groups that they too, at some point, through political struggle or negotiation, might gain a health-giving living space amenable to their own cultural practices and belief systems.

2 Urban Metabolisms and the Rise of the Global Petroleumscape

The significance of water transcended the imperative of the sanitary city. This vital liquid connected the urban to the rural, as an important element of the urban metabolism, the topic of this section. Supplying cities with food, water, and, especially, energy necessitated relationships at lager spatial scales, what urban geographers and historians often refer to as "the hinterlands." Historians, nonetheless, have neglected the global history of the urban metabolism. This history consists of colonial relationships, shared forms of modern governance, and fossil fuel-based production. Colonial and capitalist elites in the nineteenth and early twentieth centuries built, managed, and expanded urban-metabolic relations across global spaces. And they did so by means of the extraction and combustion of ever-larger quantities of fossil fuels.

In this section, I will explain the process by which fossil fuel–driven production expanded the spatial frontiers of urban metabolisms to encompass the entire world. Petroleum, in particular, given its transportability and its modifiable nature to generate derivative products, facilitated the formation of a global urban metabolism, defined here as an urban petroleumscape. Carola Hein, theorist of the petroleumscape, defines it as "a layered physical and social landscape that reinforces itself over time through human action and connects urban and rural spaces, culture and nature, materials and intangible practices" (Hein 2022: 2). I employ the petroleumscape, the spaces that connect extraction zones and sites of consumption, to illustrate and explain how this fossil fuel and the assemblage of actors who invest in it, extract it, transport it to urban markets, purchase it, and consume it have dramatically altered the global environment in general, and urban political ecologies in particular. This urban metabolism of fossil energy, which melds the cultural and the biophysical worlds, has been primarily organized through capitalist processes of commodification and accumulation, although alternative regimes of urban-metabolic governance have also been historically important. My argument here is twofold. First, the adoption of fossil energy (coal and petroleum), by unlocking industrial production and speeding up transport, radically reconstituted urban environments and the expectations of urban life. Second, while one could argue the chemical composition of petroleum, with its incredible malleability and power, enabled the global integration of cities, logistical infrastructures, and extractive hinterlands, it is important to underscore that oil investors and an assortment of state actors – both national and imperial – stitched this fossil fuel world together. But, this world was also challenged by the workers who built it and by those whose lands were dispossessed and despoiled by it throughout the twentieth-century history of empire, nation-building, and capitalist and communist models of development.

"Fossil urbanism" originated in capitalists – such as Edward Doheny of Los Angeles – seeking oil extraction opportunities in places like the Huasteca of Mexico, which themselves became new sites of urban development. This global perspective illustrates the connections between seemingly disparate energy capitals – urbanized sites of extraction and other sites of energy processing – as well as shared patterns of social, environmental, and political transformation. It also highlights the challenges and opportunities of building more sustainable cities in the Anthropocene wherein resistance to fossil productivism, the conviction that economic growth is the measure of societal prosperity – first a thoroughly capitalist objective and by the middle of the twentieth century a socialist one as well – must run through and directly challenge not only the privatized, and decidedly anti-collective, life that oil has fostered but also the vast infrastructural and logistical petroleumscape and the investments in it that reproduce daily our fossil fuel dependence.

Globalizing Urban Metabolism

Stories that tell the provenance of this or that human practice can be a fool's errand. Origins stories often stumble over terminological ambiguity regarding what counts as the specific practice under scrutiny, suffer from a myopic lens where antecedents are ignored, or base their narrative more on assumption than sound evidence. In one sense, the origin story of the urban metabolism appears obvious. For as long as there have been cities, there has been an urban metabolism. After all, cities are sites of concentrated energy brought from other places to meet basic human needs at bare minimum and surplus accumulation for a group of elites and powerholders more often than not. Yet, too often, scholars have assumed, rather anachronistically and based on limited evidence, that early urban metabolisms must have been governed by imperial leaders who violently appropriated hinterland resources to sustain growing urban populations (Mumford 1968). Recent archaeological and anthropological evidence, however, suggests that the first urban metabolisms varied widely – involving reciprocal exchanges as well as conquest and appropriation – and did not invariably entail the dispossession of land (Scott 2018; Graeber and Wengrow 2021). Regardless of the form the urban metabolism took, the spatial reach of the city remained tightly bound to extant transportation modes – human power and animal traction as well as varying kinds of water-born transport that allowed longer-distance exchanges – and thus limited.

Fast-forward several millennia to the second half of the eighteenth century, and despite wide-changing urban realities and growing proletarianization, urban metabolisms remained mostly circumscribed to the basic needs of social reproduction such as cooking, eating, and drinking. And, urban working classes frequently retained partial means of subsistence outside market relations in urban gardens and animal husbandry (Steinberg 2002; McNeur 2014; Dyl 2017; Armiero and Tucker 2017). Moreover, the technics of transport within the urban metabolism remained similarly dependent on solar energy, spatially circumscribing the reach of urban power and market exchange with surrounding resource hinterlands, although in the case of urban lighting those hinterlands included the North Atlantic Ocean ravaged by the species-extirpating whaling industry (Bolster 2014). While such urban metabolisms were culturally specific, rooted in food production practices, hydrology, and woodland cover, they were bound together by virtue of the biological imperative of the social reproduction of urban residents partially or fully lacking their own means to subsist off the land. Indeed, the conditions of spatially limited urban metabolisms led to a strikingly similar practice of nutrient recycling whereby noxious organic wastes (night soil) from humans and animals were transported for use as fertilizer by nearby farmers, who would sell or distribute their produce back to towns and cities – a historic example of an energetic circular economy (Tarr 1975; Hanley 1987; Steinberg 2002; Van Der Geest 2002; Xue 2005; Kawa 2019).

Much like the social forces of the nineteenth century effectively globalized urban-environmental governance, many of those same forces engendered a wider structural integration of the urban metabolism. First, the global-environmental imaginary, as discussed in section one, fostered a synchronous investment in large-scale hydraulic engineering that intended to more effectively control and appropriate hinterland nature (notably regional hydrological systems) but which effectively created new interdependencies between urban and rural spaces. Chicago reversed the flow of its river in a remarkable feat of engineering, sending wastewater to the Mississippi River instead of Lake Michigan from which the city pumped its drinking water (Platt 2005). Mexico City first captured water from the iconic Xochimilco springs, the bastion of Indigenous water-dependent chinampa agriculture, contributing to the desiccation of the land and its eventual urbanization. Later, the city tapped the Lerma River, part of an entirely different watershed – one of the first urban hydraulic projects to do this – and provoked Indigenous resistance to the megalopolis' expropriation of the resource that sustained their livelihoods (Perló Cohen 2012; Vitz 2018). In the urbanizing Western United States, metropolitan elites were eager to establish their cities as truly modern, and a safe and steady water supply topped the list of priorities. In 1905, for example, Los Angeles Water and Power, under the helm of its director William Mulholland, appropriated the water of Owens Valley, the story upon which the film *Chinatown* is loosely based. Less well known is the resistance some farmers mounted when their orchards and farms dried up; the aqueduct was dynamited on several occasions in the 1920s (Hundley Jr. 1992). In a story nearly as familiar, San Francisco boosters prevailed over John Muir and his preservationist allies in building a dam on the Hetch-Hetchy River, then part of Yosemite National Park, to supply the city, which was rebuilding from the devastating earthquake-fire that brought into sharp relief the city's water woes (Righter 2005). In colonial Calcutta, British sanitarians tapped the Hooghly water north of the city to supply inhabitants with drinking water, unleashing debates over the meaning of water "purity." Whereas colonial sanitarians condemned the impure Hindi practices of bathing and depositing wastes in the river, Hindi residents insisted the river was inherently pure and sacred and defended their conventional uses (Chakrabarti 2005). With urban populations booming, the global movement for sanitation remade hinterland landscapes and rural social relations and created a more technically intricate interdependence between urban and rural spaces.

Second, the enclosure and privatization of previously communal rural land by landowners and developers expanded market relations, fueling urbanization and transforming city-hinterland relationships. Stripped of their ability to live off the land, what Marx called "primitive accumulation" in his explanation of capitalism's origins, ever-larger numbers of people across colonial and neocolonial spaces between the seventeenth and twentieth centuries were compelled to purchase their means of survival by becoming wage laborers or informal vendors in cities and towns. In effect, except those who were able to cultivate urban gardens and sustain urban animal husbandry, recent urban migrants lost their "ecological autonomy" – secured through access to land, water, and forests – and became dependent on capitalist commodification to support themselves (Tutino 2007). Meanwhile remaining rural producers sought to maximize the production of foodstuffs and cooking fuel for growing urban markets. The privatization of land and the migration of landless peasants was a long, geographically uneven, and ongoing process that systematically hit the English countryside first but affected other regions quickly thereafter.

Officials in fast-growing cities, concerned about food safety, began to monitor, regulate, and often extirpate the urban subsistence practices that working-class and poor people had been able to maintain. The urban poor, especially recent migrant populations, had grown accustomed to raising their own food, a key protection from the marketization of daily reproduction needs. Raising chickens, rabbits, and pigs and tending to urban gardens occupied space and jeopardized, according to officials and elite classes, public health, order, and the aesthetic appeal of cities. Throughout the nineteenth century, city officials waged campaigns to clean up streets, which had the effect of severing the poor's urban-ecological autonomy and subsuming them further within market relations, the urban culmination of what John Bellamy Foster named the "metabolic rift" (Duffy 1990; Foster 1999; Dyl 2006; McNeur 2014; Armiero 2017). In order to maintain the healthy reproduction of urban residents, officials across the urban world also regulated cattle culling in slaughterhouses and meat quality in markets and began inspecting dairy products for contamination. Much like water quality, other goods necessary for urban social reproduction came under the purview of urban authorities who regulated the technical infrastructures built to supply cities (Smith and Phillips 2000; Pilcher 2006; Lee 2008; Aparecida Lopes 2021).

These largely synchronous developments were also accompanied by a scalar expansion. By the middle of the century, the cheap and readily available supply of coal in some areas of the world powered locomotives and steam ships, which further expanded urban-driven production across ever-vaster hinterlands. Steam-powered transport eased resource extraction for urban production and new waves of primitive accumulation, creating larger populations that depended on the market exchange of commodities. William Cronon's masterful *Nature's Metropolis* (1991) astutely follows these urban-rural connections that brought wood, wheat, meat, and other foodstuffs to the urban marketplace, transforming hinterland spaces into "second nature," spaces of commodity production and thus of capital accumulation.

Before coal powered transport and expanded urban metabolisms, it powered homes and, then, manufacturing. The story of the fossil-fuel revolution began in late sixteenth-century London where the growing cost of firewood for home heating led residents to burn coal in their furnaces. In the hundred-plus years that followed, coal increasingly drove the economy of the city and its hinterland as more and more small-scale manufacturers turned to this primary energy source and the infrastructure of coal mining, transport, and consumption exploded (Cowen 2020; Allen 2014; Nightingale 2022).

At the end of the eighteenth century, the textile capitalists of England's Lancashire region built their mills near fast-flowing rivers to run their spinning jennies, water frames, and, eventually, power looms that first industrialized textile production. These same industrialists soon found James Watt's coal-powered steam engine, the adaptation of Thomas Newcomen's original invention used to extract water from coal mines, to be enormously advantageous. The steam engine, by putting coal to work moving textile machinery, unleashed the mills' productive forces and unmoored the geography of capitalist industrialism. Andreas Malm (2016) argues that the steam engine allowed textile owners to extricate production from the limits of climate and hydrology. Mills could run equipment at any time during the year, and owners could establish larger factories in urban areas, such as Manchester, near an available workforce employed to oversee mechanized production. Coal, therefore, facilitated the exploitation of wage laborers and unlocked exponential growth in textile production, both of which demanded a corresponding acceleration of consumer and industrial goods into cities.

It is no irony that the birthplace of modern industrialism – in the textile mills around Manchester in England – soon became the heart of modern imperialism. In what one historian calls "war capitalism," textile-producing Great Britain secured, through market manipulation and warfare, the raw cotton – much of which was grown by bonded laborers – needed for the mills, and forcibly opened markets for finished British textiles (Beckert 2014). In a related global history of the urban industrialization of Europe, Sidney Mintz's classic *Sweetness and Power* (1985), examines the history of sugar, from its production on immense plantations of enslaved Africans to Europe's urban markets where workers added it to tea and coffee to sustain themselves over long work days. The rise of industrial society required the harnessing and appropriation of multiple forms of energy – the energy of slaves to pick cotton, the energy of coal to power machinery, and the caloric energy of sugar to maintain worker productivity. One historian, who places slavery squarely within energy history, makes a materially grounded argument that the transition to fossil fuels, which did ever-greater work for humans, allowed the institution of slavery to become dispensable (Nikiforuk 2012). Nonetheless, the global hinterlands of the urban-industrial metabolism during the nineteenth century were brutal places of inequality, coercion, and destruction – where once-diverse ecosystems gave way to monoculture fields of cotton and sugar. The textile mills of Manchester and the port of Liverpool, where cotton bales arrived from across the British Empire, launched a global urban-industrial revolution, founded on steam power in the factory and in modes of transport, that further expanded urban-metabolic relationships to hinterland spaces that possessed, in the words of geographer Jason Moore, "cheap nature" and "cheap energy" (Moore 2015; Patel and Moore 2017).

At the end of the nineteenth century, electricity began lighting cities, adding a new technical layer to urban metabolisms and furthering the fossil energy transition. In water-rich environments, utility providers used falling water to create electricity, and the construction of large hydro-electric dams of reinforced concrete created gigantic lakes that flooded farmland and small villages. From southeastern Canada, the Pacific Northwest and the Tennessee Valley of the United States, and central Mexico to central Ghana, Palestine, and Northern India, state officials, utility companies, and engineers trumpeted hydro-electricity as emblems of urban modernity, a basic expectation of urban life that carried promises of rural development, even if services were often deficient and development uneven at best (D'Souza 2008; Pelletier 2011; Hirst 2012; Miescher 2012; Buckley 2017; Olsson 2017; Melton 2019; Montaño 2021). As demand for electricity grew, coal, petroleum, and, eventually, natural gas powered the electrical grid more than the falling force of water. Nonetheless, numerous exceptions remained, and hydropower symbolized modernist development and furthered state projects of territorial control more readily than fossil-fuel extraction (Miescher 2012; Sutoris 2016; Pirani 2018).

The seeds of fossil urbanism were planted in England the moment large quantities of coal were shipped down rivers for domestic heating, but the global making of fossil urbanism, whereby greater numbers of urban denizens depended on fossil fuels (coal, petroleum, and natural gas) to live their daily lives, occurred over many decades, if not centuries. Christopher Jones (2014) takes the fossil fuel-rich mid-Atlantic region of the United States during the nineteenth century as his case study to explain how cities transitioned to fossil fuels for their energy needs. Jones argues that urban dependence on fossil fuels and fossil-powered electricity came about not because of immediate consumer preference but because coal and oil investors designed the transport networks – the canals, railroads, transmission wires, and oil pipelines – between 1830 and 1930 that linked urban centers to the oil fields of Western Pennsylvania and the coal veins throughout the state. Once in urban markets, capitalists manipulated prices and advertised their products to secure consumers, both domestic and industrial. The dependence of cities on fossil fuels emerged, according to Jones, through a "set of positive feedback loops . . . between the building of infrastructure, the economic investments in these systems, the action of human agents, and new consumption practices" (8), despite initial resistance from consumers who remained stubbornly attached to fuelwood. As consumer demand increased, companies expanded transport networks, enabling more intensive and extensive extraction. Meanwhile, a larger supply of fossil fuels led to fossil energy-created electricity, which, in turn, allowed industrialists to employ mobile machinery that received power from an outlet rather than from the fires of direct fossil fuel combustion.

By the 1920s, mid-Atlantic urban residents from Baltimore to New York City could no longer thrive in, let alone imagine, a world without coal and oil. The steady and cheap transport of coal and petroleum created new energy demands (lighting, transport, industrial production). It transformed older needs such as cooking and heating as well as industrial uses like iron smelting in ways that permitted urban population growth that otherwise, with wood energy, would have required massive amounts of land. And, it permitted factory siting in existing population centers (Jones 2014).

The transition from an organic energy regime to a fossil energy regime, in short, made large-scale global urbanization possible. And while Jones' narrative focuses on one crucial fast-urbanizing region of this energy transition, similar developments occurred in roughly synchronous fashion around the world, although less markedly in colonized spaces, which lacked energy sovereignty. Indeed, nation-state competition drove fossil urbanism forward. Witnessing the coal-powered urban industrialization taking place in England, Prussian elites of the Ruhr Valley dug their own coal mines, and Philadelphia's coal boosters imagined a future similar to England's. Chemist and coal enthusiast Thomas Cooper remarked: "In this country every suggestion that brings forward the importance of coal to the public view is of moment . . . . All, all the superior wealth, power and energy of Great Britain, is founded on her coal mining" (Jones 2014: 27). In a sense, the positive feedback loops that Jones identifies for the mid-Atlantic were global, spurred by the interaction of liberal narratives that equated large cities with civilization, industrial growth with progress, and private profit with prosperity. Fossil fuels fit capitalism's growth imperative impeccably, and given their geographical dispersion over the earth's surface, nation-states, empires, and fossil capitalists raced to secure these power-dense energy resources. They worked to expand their energy hinterlands domestically and through imperial conquest, and deliver them to a wide range of urban consumers and factories (Yergin 1991; Pavilack 2011; Young 2015; Vergara 2021; Kiddle 2021; Black 2021).

The industrial energy metabolisms of Sao Paulo and Mexico City, two of the vanguard cities of Latin American industrialization, illustrate this dynamic well. At the end of the nineteenth century, industrialists drew on their immediate energy hinterlands for water and wood power. For example, the destruction of the Atlantic Forest of Brazil had much to do with Sao Paulo's energy needs. As these organic energy forms dwindled and as industrial and urban consumer demands escalated, investors turned to coal and later petroleum, drawing on more distant national hinterlands (Mexico) and international hinterlands (Sao Paulo) (Brannstrom 2005; Acker 2020; Vergara 2021).

Urban-industrial metabolisms – the electricity, water supply, drainage, food, and fossil fuels that sustained urban growth – demanded the construction of complex technical systems that spanned regions and frontiers. Historian Chris Otter has labeled these overlapping technical systems the global technosphere (Otter 2017). Perhaps no other aspect of the global technosphere has been more physically prominent and socially and ecologically consequential than the one built to extract, convey, and distribute petroleum and its derivative products.

The Global Petroleumscape

In 1890, Mexico's Huasteca region, located in the tropical lowlands of northern Veracruz and southern Tamaulipas along the Gulf of Mexico, was a tropical jungle peppered with cattle ranches and Totonac Indigenous communities who lived from hunting and subsistence agriculture. That year the first rail line connecting the small port city of Tampico to the central highlands opened, and the city served as a hub of Mexico's new export-driven commerce (Kueker 2008). Three decades later, two oil companies (Huasteca Petroleum and Mexican Eagle Petroleum) devastated wetland and forest ecosystems, erected dozens of oil rigs and pipelines, and turned Tampico into one of the first oil towns outside of the United States, a small city populated by migrants from the central highlands who had settled in worker camps.

If we were to follow Huastecan crude from point of extraction to the point of consumption, the story might have gone something like this. Pumped by workers from the fields outside Tampico, the crude would have flowed through a pipeline to the port where a tanker ship would have brought it to a refining facility in urbanizing coastal Texas. Once refined there – and let us imagine the end product was gasoline and not fuel oil or bitumen – it would have flowed through another network of pipes into a storage facility and finally to a gas station. There, a station attendant would have pumped the gasoline into a vehicle, perhaps a Ford Model T, which may have allowed a resident of an American metropolis to purchase a home in one of the new subdivisions emerging outside city centers.

This story of Huastecan crude embodies the emerging global petroleums-cape. But, why not talk about a global urban coalscape as well? After all, it was coal that accelerated the global urban-industrial revolution and the transportation of raw materials and other goods in and out of metropoles. It was coal that untethered industrial output from the vagaries and contingencies of hydro-logical flows and the geography of water and thus allowed urban factory siting. Nonetheless, this fossil fuel did not have the global technical and commercial impact on the urban process and form as petroleum would have at the beginning of the twentieth century. To be sure, once steam power was employed in commercial and navy ships, transoceanic access to coal and the infrastructure of coaling stations at strategic ports became an essential imperial priority (Shulman 2015; Khalili 2020). Yet coal did not spur the development of a massive global technical infrastructure that crisscrossed urban spaces. Coal and urbanization remained largely nation-specific phenomena. The soot and smog produced by burning coal led to smoke-abatement movements among Progressive-era reformers on both sides of the Atlantic, damaging coal's reputation as a source of energy (Stradling 1999; Uekötter 2009). But the drawbacks of coal ran much deeper than environmental and aesthetic norms. The physical properties of coal played a major role in limiting its ease of transport and its uses, and the social relations wrapped up in its commodity chain – from extraction to point of consumption in cities – proved disadvantageous in relation to petroleum, the other major fossil fuel vying for urban markets. Timothy Mitchell argues in *Carbon Democracy* (2011) that coal, as a solid energy form, required huge numbers of workers to dig it up and transport it to urban and industrial markets, whereas petroleum extraction was more amenable to mechanization and its transportation eased via automated pipelines, large tanker ships, and mechanized storage facilities. The chokepoints in coal-driven capitalism, Mitchell argues, afforded workers incredible leverage to shut down industrial production and win important demands (including workplace protections, the right to unionize, and the right to vote) from ruling classes across North America and Western Europe. Once again, however, fossil-fueled capitalism resolved a labor dilemma in its favor. One fossil fuel empowered workers; the other disempowered them, according to Mitchell. Although Mitchell exaggerated the degree to which oil-based industrialization allowed the capitalist class to temper worker power in cities and extraction sites (as we shall see, oil workers flexed their political muscle too), its ease of transport and the variegated products refining technologies could produce – gasoline, kerosene, jet fuel, liquefied petroleum gas, diesel, fuel oil, and so on – made a new global landscape.

A Global History of the Petroleumscape

Since energy studies emerged several decades ago, encompassing history, political science, anthropology, and related humanistic disciplines, there has been an outpouring of scholarship about "black gold." Much of this work addresses energy transitions, the lived experience of oil, and political economy – either from the position of the infamous "resource curse," which confers upon oil a seemingly magical agency to inevitably corrupt and centralize power, or, alternatively, what might be called the empire-capitalism-petroleum triad (Yergin 1991; Coronil 1997; Smil 1994; Seiferle and Osmann 2010; Mitchell 2011; Ross 2012; Watts 2012; Appel et al. 2015; Khalili 2020; Black 2021). Apart from studies of automobility, the field of urban studies has paid less attention to the diverse ways petroleum has shaped urbanization over time (Sheller and Urry 2000; Wolfe 2010; Wells 2014). My purpose here is to bring the concept of the "petroleumscape" to urban history in order to center the relationship between the built environment of petroleum and urban cultural, political, and ecological transformations. The planetary urbanization that some urban scholars proclaim may be somewhat hyperbolic, but it would be impossible to comprehend the scale of urbanization and its global qualities over the last century and a half without examining the flows and connections inherent in the most crucial of all urban-industrial metabolisms: petroleum energy.

Four historical themes encapsulate the urban dimensions of the global petroleumscape. First, the urban history of petroleum transcends spaces of extraction and consumption to include the networked infrastructures that link the two, or to paraphrase one urban geographer – the logistical cities in the petroleumscape (Cowen 2020; Simpson 2022). Second, the urban impacts of petroleum extend beyond the familiar physical infrastructure to include a set of ancillary activities derived from large profits. From the very beginning of the industry, petroleum executives have funneled the surplus capital of petroleum production into urbanization, often with the intention to reinforce the petroleumscape. Third, oil companies and oil-backed states, particularly in colonial and neocolonial contexts, made profitable centers of extraction and refining through the spatial control and segregation of a diverse range of workers, generating in the process new forms of environmental inequality and precariousness. Workers, experiencing harsh and toxic conditions at home in segregated camps and in the workplace, organized and resisted, sometimes to redress environmental and health concerns. Fourth, these diverse political struggles over the petroleumscape, in combination with the geopolitics of the world energy system and patterns of surplus reinvestment in petroleum-producing countries, have led to a diverse and idiosyncratic set of petroleum-based political cultures in cities around the world.

The Logistical Petroleumscape

Over the last decade, energy historians, historians of the built environment, and geographers – influenced by Michael Watts and Hannah Appel's concept of the "oil assemblage" – have highlighted the impacts of the circulation and delivery of petroleum on urban social relations and ecologies (Appel et al. 2015). Since the 1860s, colonial and national states and private oil companies have forged "logistical cities" that specialize in the refining and circulation of petroleum. The petroleum infrastructures – of pipelines, railroad hubs, refineries, storage facilities, petrochemical facilities, ports, and harbors – of these cities and entire regions are crucial to understanding the transformations of urban power relations, the formation of urban-environmental inequalities, unequal national economic development as well as the relations between global centers and peripheries.

Since the first oil booms along Oil Creek in Western Pennsylvania and in the Baku region of Imperial Russia, urban power relations have flowed literally through petroleum. Standard Oil built many of the first refineries in Cleveland, Pittsburgh, and Philadelphia, and then in the infamous "Cleveland Massacre" of 1872 proceeded to monopolize oil refining and rail transportation across the mid-Atlantic. Standard Oil's control of the urban petroleumscape cemented a practice of global oil development in which large corporate and state oil players wielded political and financial power over urban space to foster petroleum production and circulation.

Carola Hein (2018) traces the development of the vast physical infrastructure of refining, storage, and transport between Antwerp and Rotterdam, the world's second greatest concentration of petroleum facilities, bested only by the Gulf Coast of the United States. This regional petroleumscape developed alongside the growing diversity of refined products, starting with kerosene for illumination and followed by gasoline, asphalt, and fuel oil. Hein shows how powerful municipal and oil players – both domestic and international – appropriated rural space and coastlines for the construction of ports, rails and roads, refineries, and storage facilities. A convenient geographical location with rail and water transport connections allowed for the easy delivery of refined products that by the 1950s increasingly came from the Middle East. This coastal region, still unknowingly regarded by some as a bucolic landscape of farms and windmills, became Europe's center of petroleum refining, storage, and transport, and a major conurbation in its own right (Hein 2018).

While Hein's work is useful in visualizing the spatial components of the petroleumscape, other scholars have more directly addressed the political ecology of these logistical cities. Laleh Khalili (2020) tracks the urban spatial changes and ecological degradation that Middle Eastern rulers, operating within an unequal global economy, unleashed during the twentieth century to facilitate the shipment and processing of vast quantities of crude oil. They built new ports, often at a distance from traditional urban cores (Kuwait City's massive petroleum refining and port infrastructure is an example of this) and deepened harbors in existing urban centers to handle crude oil exports, shipped via increasingly large oil tankers. In the 1930s and 1940s, under King Abdulaziz, the Saudi Arabian government dredged harbors that transformed the small fishing villages of Ras Tanura and Damman into deep-sea ports. The ports served as nodes of distribution to take crude that had arrived by pipeline and rail from Saudi oil fields and also as points to disembark machinery and raw materials used to build worker cities and administrative headquarters.

The practices and physical spaces that eased the flow of oil across global space had devastating social and environmental consequences. Dredging wreaked havoc on marine ecosystems and imperiled fishing economies around the two bourgeoning port cities in the 1960s and 1970s. Developers used the excavated sediment and combined it with locally quarried gravel and sand to create new land, further altering coastal environments and destroying mangrove forests, mudflats, and coastal wetlands. Meanwhile, oil tankers frequently spilled crude and refined products during loading and unloading and tossed overboard petroleum-contaminated ballast water, compounding the degradation of marine life (Kahlili 2020). Assessing the transformations in the Persian Gulf and the Red Sea, Kahlili writes (80): "so much has been changed in that space where land and sea meet, so many shorelines shifted, seabeds lifted, hills levelled, and lands claimed, that very little remains of the coastline that fishermen, pearl-divers, sailors, and merchants of the eighteenth or even nineteenth centuries could recognize."

The story of environmental deterioration and toxicity within this logistical landscape was not limited to so-called Third World contexts. The history of oil drilling in Los Angeles is well known, and even today one only needs to take a ride in an automobile to see the derricks that pepper the urban landscape. The Los Angeles of the storage and shipping of petroleum products is less well known.

The oil boom of the 1920s in the Los Angeles basin and as far away as Kern County in the Central Valley led oil companies to expand port infrastructure and erect huge storage facilities, railroad hubs, and pipelines along the coast between Long Beach and San Pedro. The new logistical landscape, erected to store and move hundreds of thousands of barrels of oil every day, produced not only durable coastal changes but also short-term disasters and chronic pollution. In September 1923, a fire engulfed the harbor, burned 500,000 barrels of oil, and endangered thousands. *The Los Angeles Times* blamed a disgruntled unemployed worker associated with the militant labor union International Workers of the World for the fire, but the true cause remains unknown. Everyday pollution was more insidious. According to one report, "the sea lanes from Los Angeles to Panama became a veritable procession of tankers," and this constant movement of surplus oil through the harbor resulted in frequent collisions and accidents (Cooke 2017: 79). By 1923, because of its role in shipping surplus oil out of southern California, Los Angeles overtook San Francisco as the leading port on the Pacific Coast (Cooke 2017).

To the north in Vancouver, which has served as a logistical hub of petroleum for all of Western Canada since the 1950s, the urban-environmental transform-ation was not as dramatic, but just as detrimental to Indigenous peoples who had subsisted off lands and waters. The Indigenous peoples of British Colombia have mounted numerous protests over the ongoing development of Vancouver as a logistical petroleum city (Cowen 2020; Simpson 2022).

In all of these urban-industrial logistical landscapes, pollution was rampant and largely uncontrolled, regardless of the location. In studying Houston and its petroleum-drenched Gulf surroundings, several scholars have documented the pollution of land, water, and air directly caused by company refineries, storage facilities, and shipping that gave Houston the notorious title of "oil pollution capital of America." As Joseph Pratt states, pollution affected multiple points of the delivery and refining operation, from the sulfuric emissions of refineries to spillages of oil itself into land and water – "from pipeline to storage tank, from tank to refinery, from refinery to loading docks, from docks to tankers" (Pratt 2007; Gorman 2007). For these scholars, however, the political focus is not one of capitalist extraction and trade, colonial power structures, or Native resistance but rather of an active civil society petitioning for government regulations of an industry that preached self-regulation and growth at all costs.

Financial Reinvestment and the Urban Form

From the very beginning of our age of petroleum, oil executives have reinvested profits in cities. First, oil companies have sited corporate headquarters in strategic city center locations, such as Houston, Caracas, and Kuwait City, where they occupy large expanses of real estate and, oftentimes, form a crucial part of civic pride and identity. Second, oil capitalists have made significant donations, often disconnected from controversial company names, to educational institutions such as Harvard and the University of Chicago, as well as to cultural centers and museums around the world, attracting new residents, skilled laborers, and tourists to certain metropolises. Third, oil companies built worker housing and worker educational facilities, some of which helped create decent-sized cities in their own right (Santiago 2006; Tinker Salas 2009; Fucarro 2009; Fucarro 2022; Hein 2022).

Petroleum profits have flowed into, and altered, urban spaces in less noticeable, but possibly more profound, ways that are less clearly connected to energy capital than the examples listed above. In Los Angeles, at the end of the nineteenth century, transnational investors paired city and empire-building by investing in land and mineral resources across the southern border with Mexico and in urban development at home (Kim 2019). For our purposes here, the Los Angeles-Mexico connection exemplified the incipient global urban petroleumscape, forged within a regime of racial segregation. Edward Doheny was one of the oil investors who made Southern California, and Los Angeles proper, among the first major producers of petroleum at the turn of the century. He transferred, like investors before and after him, racialized labor regimes to the tropical Huasteca region during the first two decades of the twentieth century, where his oil fields under the Huasteca Petroleum Company were among the most productive in the world. In fact, the company's Cerro Azul Number 4 well became the world's most prolific by 1915, producing more oil than all of California's wells combined. Doheny's company not only led to rapid and environmentally toxic urbanization around Mexico's oil fields, but the wealth he brought back fueled LA's own segregated and environmentally hazardous urban development. Doheny's Mexican oil wealth allowed him to further develop the city's oil industry, whose infrastructure and rigs often were (and remain) located adjacent to residences. He also helped establish Chester Palace, the city's first gated community, and invested heavily in the development of Beverly Hills (Kim 2019). Doheny's operations exemplified how investments in global energy hinterlands and reinvestments in urban spaces helped build two of the world's first energy capitals, to borrow Joseph Pratt's term, Los Angeles and Tampico, cities that exemplified cutthroat capitalism and racialized labor control.

Staying in the western United States, the oil capitalist Ralph Loyd funneled profits from oil development in LA, Ventura, and San Joaquin counties into a set of commercial real estate development interests along Wilshire Boulevard in Los Angeles and, most importantly, in Portland, Oregon. There, he contributed to the suburbanization of the city, with automobile-friendly LA serving as his model (Adamson 2018). Commercial and residential urban real estate were seen as safe havens to park the surplus value extracted from energy hinterlands, and in the case of urbanization in the Western United States, contributed to an automobile-centered culture.

Decades before California's oil barons developed the oil fields and cities of the American west, Muslim investors in the rich oil fields of Baku, in competition with the Nobel Brothers Oil Company, the Russian equivalent of Standard Oil, reinvested their wealth in the city to promote a Muslim urban modernity. Thanks to the urban vision of Taghiyev and other oil developers who made the city the top world producer of oil by 1900, Baku soon gained the moniker of the "Paris of the Caspian," with wide boulevards, esplanades, parks, electricity, cultural institutions, and "bombastic palaces" (Blau 2018).

Modernist urban planning sprang from multiple social forces, including left-wing movements and ideologies and bourgeois reformist impulses for order and beauty amid a rapidly changing world. The physical changes to the land brought on by oil development and flows of oil capital within urban circuits of power, however, also shaped planning history. For example, the planners of Baku, influenced by incipient German industrial planning, created new zoning laws and a buffer zone between industrial and residential-commercial development as early as the 1870s (Blau 2018). Baku represented the first of many oil-soaked cities that were planned by public authorities rather than strictly by oil companies or oil-dependent real estate interests. Yet, oil revenue, company priorities, and state objectives of constructing political legitimacy through monumental works saturated the urbanization process. The built environments of Kuwait City, Abu Dhabi, Dubai, Lagos, and Caracas reflect these priorities, as major metropolises built to showcase a petroleum modernity of prosperity, order, and habitability – albeit with varying degrees of success (Gandy 2006; Tinker Salas 2009; Al-Nakib 2015; Hein 2022). This phenomenon crossed geopolitical Cold War boundaries: Soviet planners sought to showcase the modernist development of Baku along socialist principles of collective worker housing, ample green space, and transport connectivity, even as the wanton placement of (often leaky) pipelines and other oil infrastructure cut through neighborhoods and public housing (Blau 2018; Crawford 2022). Even Le Corbusier's modernist radiant city design and the International Congress of Modern Architecture (CIAM) planning movement, friendly to the automobile and asphalt-paved roadways, was supported by Standard Oil and other companies (Hein 2010). Historical studies of the urban built environment, soaked in oil physically, financially, and symbolically, would benefit from a full consideration of the financial and political investments of global petroleum players.

The investments in the logistical circuits of petroleum and the urban rein-vestments of surplus oil revenue, together, have shaped the political economy of the global petroleumscape. It is crucial to think comparatively across broadly synchronic patterns of petroleum-driven urban industrialization and consider the ways internal (that is, national) racial power structures have intersected with fossil energy regimes to create different levels of material prosperity. Energy historian Germán Vergara points to the causative relationship between the siting of pipelines, refineries, and other fossil fuel infrastructure, on the one hand, and the levels of urban prosperity and industrial development that fossil fuels, especially petroleum, fostered across central and northern Mexico, on the other (Vergara 2021) (see Figure 2). Mexico's petroleumscape was not an accident of geography but itself a product of decades, if not centuries, of uneven economic development and a racial regime that favored the putative rationality of mestizaje and whiteness in northern and central Mexico over the irrationality and backwardness of Mexico's Indigenous south. While there is a general dearth of work on this aspect of the global petroleumscape, we might consider the energetic bases of unequal regional and national development in other nation-states with their own historical fossil fuel reserves. In Brazil, the industrializing south was supplied with petroleum from the poorer Afro-Brazilian north around

Figure 2 Tina Modotti, Oil Tank, 1927. Located in central Mexico.
Digital Image © The Museum of Modern Art/Licensed by SCALA / Art
Resource, NY

Salvador in the middle of the twentieth century (Hein 2010; Acker 2020). And, across the Arabian Peninsula, the interior extractive hinterlands have supplied the wealth that has accrued to petro-oligarchies in places such as Bahrain, Dubai, and Abu Dhabi.

The Urban Political Ecologies of Segregated Worker Camps on the Oil Frontiers

We now turn our attention to these extractive hinterlands, located predominantly in colonized and neocolonized spaces after WWI. The inhabitants of these urban spaces, small towns abruptly transformed into cosmopolitan, if radically unequal, urban centers, tended to experience the most severe ecological devastation. In these spaces, oil companies created segregated urban environments amid highly exploitative and dangerous labor conditions. Workers and nationalist groups challenged these colonial and neocolonial relationships, reshaping social relations within the global petroleumscape.

The American and European oil prospectors who scoured deserts and tropical jungles for black gold brought with them ideas of progress and production techniques that made for remarkably similar urban trajectories. For the oilmen of the early twentieth century, these foreign lands of tropical America and the arid deserts of the Middle East were forlorn and abandoned, waiting for the so-called progressive and rational initiatives of white men like themselves. Oil embodied progress and prosperity for all: Edward Doheny remarked, with no sense of irony, that his industry had turned Tampico into "one of the happiest communities of any city in the world" (Santiago 2010: 173). The workers, to put it generously, did not agree. Work in the oil fields and in construction was backbreaking, hot, dangerous, and toxic. Recent scholarship on oil workers and their settlement patterns permits a much more global, diachronic, and comprehensive understanding of the ecologies of oil urbanization.

In Iran, Iraq, Mexico, and Venezuela, companies drew on decades of experience in racist enclave mining in the United States and colonial segregation practices elsewhere to erect exclusive encampments for foreign managers, leaving workers to fend for themselves in unhealthy spaces (Vitalis 2009). Because of the near-total lack of transportation infrastructure to early well sites, workers, regardless of status and skill, generally built makeshift homes with locally available material on lands adjacent to polluting wells, derricks, and refineries. The toxic work environments, therefore, were also toxic living environments, located in flood- and disease-prone areas and lacking sanitary services (Santiago 2006; Tinker Salas 2009; Elling 2015). Workers regularly inhaled toxic fumes, dragged oil into their neighborhoods and homes, and feared the omnipresent threat of fire and noxious gases from ruptured wells and storage tanks. In the town of Ambrosio near Lake Maracaibo in Venezuela, for example, a Gulf Oil well caught fire only 50 meters from the main street, killing several people and panicking hundreds of others. Two devastating fires ripped through another Venezuelan oil boom town in 1928 and in 1929; the first destroyed up to 80 percent of the town (Kozlof 2004; Santiago 2006; Tinker Salas 2009).

Meanwhile, executives and privileged foreign workers enjoyed fully serviced subdivisions and homes often modeled on their homelands – in most cases Southern California-style homes with citrus gardens, neatly patterned palm trees, green lawns, and picket fences or English-style homes surrounded by begonia gardens (Santiago 2006; Tinker Salas 2009; Bet Shlimon 2013; Blau 2015). A visitor to ARAMCO's oil town at Dhaharan, Saudi Arabia in 1945 remarked that "it was just like a bit of U.S.A – modern air conditioned houses, swimming pool, movie theater, etc" (Vitalis 2009: 80). These were the typical landscapes of urban inequality in which foreign enclaves free of toxicity and disease were separated from worker settlements. And these oil enclaves for foreign managers continue to this day, as evidenced by recent oil development in Equatorial Guinea where Texan managers' and technicians' families reside within the walled residential and business compounds of Malabo (Appel 2012).

Working-class and nationalist consciousness followed the petroleum extraction frontiers. In the residential camps and worksites of Veracruz at the beginning of the twentieth century, Mexican oil workers organized to redress pollution and toxic conditions (Santiago 2006). Other oil worker struggles may not have confronted the ecology of oil labor as directly as Mexico's workers did. However, broader concerns over the landscape of inequality in the urban petroleumscape – from inferior housing and segregated camps to high costs of living – permeated workers' movements (Vitalis 2009; Tinker Salas 2009; Bet Shlimon 2013; Blau 2015; Elling 2015; Atabaki 2018). These movements generally bolstered nationalist and anti-imperial politics, and the threat of expropriation, consummated in Mexico (1938), Iran (briefly in 1951), Libya (under Gaddafi in the early 1970s), and in Venezuela (1976), loomed over oil capitalists.

The risks these movements posed to companies' bottom lines and investments compelled them to employ a mixture of wage concessions, housing investments, surveillance, increased automation, and, to divide workers, more comprehensive ethnic and nation-based segregation policies. They invested in settling workers into camps that supported better housing either for rent or for purchase, commissaries with price controls, and more comprehensive services such as electricity, sewerage, water supply, and transportation (Tinker Salas 2009; Bet Shlimon 2013; Atabaki 2018). In some instances, companies also decided to invest in municipal services that went well beyond the immediate needs of their workers, as was the case in Kirkuk following the 1946 worker strike (Bet Shlimon 2013). The new company-built worker camps, nonetheless, not only remained segregated from the upper-echelon workforce but also, in a classic divide-and-conquer strategy, served to further segregate workers by nationality and ethnicity and submit them to new forms of surveillance (Fucarro 2009). In the oil-rich town of Abadan, Iran, for example, company and municipal planners established separate neighborhoods for migrant Indians and Native Iranians, who occupied different ranks in the labor hierarchy, and distanced them from British employees who perceived them as racially inferior and more prone to disease. Ahmadabad housed the lower ranks of workers who were predominantly Iranian. The workers' squatter neighborhood, full of shanties and unsanitary huts, was equipped with a rudimentary sewer system and a water system of public fountains. The British camp comprised "spacious villas, neatly manicured lawns, clean streets, and full infrastructure of modern amenities and entertainment." The company constructed an intermediate neighborhood, replete with basic urban services and formal housing units, to shelter Indian migrant laborers and serve as a buffer between British managers and Native workers. These Indian migrant workers occupied the middle rung of the oil labor hierarchy, taking up jobs in company administrative offices. In this unequal petroleumscape, the company ensured that "even the public spaces within and between neighborhoods were often segregated," including drinking fountains, libraries, and hospitals (Elling 2015: 207–208). This racial segregation of work and residence exacerbated sectarian and ethnic tensions, resulting in occasional outbreaks of urban violence in some oil cities (Elling 2015; Ghrawi 2015; Bet Shlimon 2019; Atabaki 2019).

Across the border in Kirkuk, Iraq, the Iraq Petroleum Company, a business with majority Anglo-Iranian Company stakes, established towns along the pipeline. Company officials housed the most skilled local workers in Arrapha estate's "grey stone residential buildings, with tree-lined avenues … recreational facilities, administrative offices, schools and supermarkets" (Fuccarro 2015: 228) The "unskilled" workers who toiled in the oil fields populated informal neighborhoods in the fast-growing Kirkuk, similar to those of Ahmadabad, although some, following the 1946 oil strike, received company housing within Kirkuk's Arrapha. European management, meanwhile, settled in the exclusive and spacious "New Camp" (Fuccarro 2015). In a quest to quell labor militancy, provide comfortable and familiar enclaves for their foreign workers, and manage seemingly chaotic urban environments, petroleum companies across the Global South between the 1920s and 1950s established what might be called the modular oil city – of segregated camps, services, and neighborhoods by rank and nationality.

This modular oil urbanization in extraction areas in the early and mid-twentieth century was capitalist to its core. However, inter-state competition fostered a shared élan for oil-driven development that transcended ideological divides during the Cold War. In post-revolutionary China, the urban development of the oil fields of Daqing in the cold northeast of the country reflected the Maoist ideology of the Chinese state and the political imperatives brought on by the Great Leap forward-induced famine. The early boom years of 1959 and 1960 followed a familiar pattern of the first oil strikes in Persia, Mexico, and Venezuela. Thousands of migrants flocked to the area for work in the fields, settling in similarly dangerous locations adjacent to new oil wells as their counterparts in the capitalist world had, since transportation was rudimentary or nonexistent. State officials then planned to build out Daqing as a modern industrial city along Soviet lines, as had been done in Baku, but those plans quickly vanished when party leaders emphasized rural resettlement due to food production woes. Yet Maoist planners, further motivated to develop the Daqing oil fields once the split with the Soviet Union threatened foreign supplies, designed Daqing to close the "three great gaps of revolutionary China" – mental versus manual labor, urban versus rural, and agricultural versus industrial. The result was a unique form of the oil city, a decentralized urbanism intent on closing the "metabolic rift" (Hou 2018: 85–105. See also Boland 2016). The vast oil fields were surrounded by worker-peasant villages that combined farming, conducted by the women, and labor in the oil industry, conducted mostly by the men. Farm and factory fused together in Daqing through the reproduction of traditional gender roles. Unlike the market relations that prevailed in capitalist company towns, the Chinese state offered inexpensive or fully decommodified cradle-to-grave services in the villages. And, although skilled workers enjoyed less dangerous working conditions, they mostly lived in the same type of housing, fully if often rudimentarily serviced, and were obligated to work in the fields for their first couple of years of service (Hou 2018). In post-revolutionary China, Daqing's decentralized urbanism, while hardly a utopia given the harsh labor conditions and austere living conditions, served as a paragon for industrial development elsewhere in China during the 1960s and 1970s. Planners deliberately juxtaposed this decentralized urbanism against both Soviet and capitalist models of urban industrialization (Hou 2018). Although the two urban-industrial models in oil extraction zones were radically different in terms of their ideological foundation and their social relations, there were some broadly similar patterns. Companies and state officials used worker housing to discipline the workforce, and in oil-producing countries everywhere, national elites promoted domestic petroleum extraction as a lever of economic development and a symbol of national sovereignty.

Petroleum Cultures and Urban Political Horizons

For over a century, oil companies, political elites, and other oil-reliant sectors of industrial capital have pushed narratives in which petroleum symbolizes some combination of freedom and material prosperity. This association has been strongest in the United States, where the automobile, concomitant with suburbanization, became synonymous with individual freedom and fostered a "privatized life" antagonistic to urban commons in transport and housing (Sheller and Urry 2000; Robbins 2012; Huber 2013). However, the United States does not hold exclusive rights to the culture of petroleum. Here, I discuss global petroleum cultures, embedded in, and respondent to, urban social relations and physical landscapes.

Nations such as Brazil, Chile, and Mexico, as well as most of those of Western Europe, joined the United States in its beatification of the automobile, which represented industrial modernity, middle-class status, and freedom of movement (Wolfe 2010; Booth 2013; Vergara 2021). The oil industry, automobile companies, and tourism agencies promoted the open road and the individual freedom and prosperity of privatized transport on newly asphalt-paved roads across the urban capitalist world in the twentieth century, although in some of these places automobility remained a privilege of the few and in others large investments in urban and regional public transit tempered the culture of automobility.

In the Communist bloc countries, urban development, which revolved more around collective goods and dense multifamily modernist housing, tended to depend less on the automobile (French and Hamilton 1979; Bittner 1998; Logan 2021). Still, many citizens of Soviet-bloc countries aspired to car ownership as a marker of status and Western individual freedom, and the "socialist car culture" that resulted was a product of negotiations with reluctant state authorities who considered the automobile a threat to collective life (Sigelbaum 2012). Meanwhile, party leaders and state officials throughout the Communist bloc promoted their own version of a petroleum culture, one in which access to cheap petroleum, from China or the Soviet Union, would catapult their nations into a socialist industrial modernity, a kind of technological utopia to outpace capitalist production (Sigelbaum 2008; Hou 2018). Indeed, starting in the 1920s, Soviet oil production was among the world's highest, and Soviet oil exports to Communist bloc countries were critical in maintaining political allegiance. And residents of the Third world saw in oil, once wrested from foreign hands, the promise of turbocharged development held back by neocolonialism while left-leaning governments also saw in 'black gold" an opportunity to redistribute wealth to the working classes. (Coronil 1997; Al-Nakib 2015).

The connection between petroleum and a specifically urban idea of prosperity transcended national and geopolitical boundaries. Cheap and free-flowing petroleum into growing cities, it was understood, laid the foundation for prosperity, and a diverse set of otherwise ideologically opposed political elites understood the basic metabolic function of petroleum in sustaining an urban way of life. Just as Nixon's "energy czar" appointee William Simon asserted that this "unique commodity" was "the lifeblood of our economy," Arab nationalists understood oil in similar metabolic terms: "Petroleum ... is to the world as blood is to the human body, and both would expire without them. In this simile, an oilfield might be likened to a human heart" (Huber 2013: 115; Fucarro 2022: 135).

These narratives of petroleum-defined freedom and prosperity seem to have been rather solid across the globe in the twentieth century, but even before the climate movement shined a spotlight on fossil fuel combustion, workers and other inhabitants within the global petroleumscape have, in some times and places, challenged such associations. Political discourses excoriating environmental injustice, ecological damage, and state malfeasance have competed with, and sometimes overwhelmed, the narratives of prosperity and freedom. Indigenous peoples, mostly from the outskirts of oil-soaked cities and towns, have spearheaded anti-extractivist campaigns for territorial sovereignty and ecological protection, from Ecuador and Nigeria to Western Canada, and beyond (Sawyer 2004; Allen 2006; Watts 2008; Auyero and Swinstun 2009; Sellers 2012; Sanzana Calvet and Castán Broto 2020; Simpson 2022). The extent to which oil workers themselves (and other urbanites) have historically participated in properly urban-environmental justice struggles remains an open question. The Mexican oil workers in Veracruz challenged "the ecology of oil," as previously discussed, but they were not alone. In oil-boom Los Angeles in the 1920s, the typical oil worker-conservationist divide that came to prevail in the United States, if not beyond, did not obtain. Working-class residents, many of whom toiled in the oil industry, of communities between Huntington Beach and Torrance (including the logistical networks of Long Beach and the Los Angeles harbor) organized trade unions that preached conservation and denounced the oil companies' reckless destruction of their neighborhoods. Union organizers regularly decried "the evils of overproduction, profligate waste, and pollution." Local labor leader Fred Jackson, who was especially vociferous against oil pollution, rhetorically asked if the new oil towns were turning into places "'for teeming, toiling human life, covered with dust, dirt, and oil'" (Quam-Wickam 1998: 199, 197). Homeowners joined the chorus of dissent. The residents of Venice Beach, witnessing the devastation caused by gushers and the eyesores of derricks in their neighborhoods, led a reformist campaign to protect their property, the beauty of their communities, and the incipient beachfront tourism of southern California.

Environmentally motivated worker struggles were not limited to the early unregulated and hyper-exploitative period of oil development in the United States. Fast-forward to the 1970s when Toni Mazzochi, the leader of the Oil, Chemical, and Atomic Workers Union, took up Fred Jackson's campaign for worker health and justice. Mazzochi, who ascertained the interlocking relationship between capital's exploitation of nature and labor, led worker–community campaigns against toxic and dangerous workplaces and neighborhoods, especially across the petroleum-refining South, helping to usher in both the Occupational Safety and Health Administration (OSHA) and the Environmental Protection Agency's Superfund program (Leopold 2007; Estabrook, Levenstein, and Wooding 2018). These traditions of worker–community coalition building have also animated more recent environmental justice struggles in the urban areas of central Louisiana, known as "cancer ally" to activists because of its high concentration of polluting petrochemical complexes (Allen 2006).

Protests over the ecological damage and environmental injustice in the urban petroleumscape, however, have been blunted by a particular oil rationality, most notable where oil workers have attained a higher social status – as an "aristocracy of labor" – and where the promise of oil revenue redistribution has been strongest. Most oil workers' unions, even those independent of state control, regularly pursue further extraction and the more equitable distribution of its fruits (Valdivia and Benavides 2018; Jafari 2018). Nonetheless, for many, living with oil creates a political culture of ambivalence. Some residents of the urban petroleumscape neither strictly oppose nor consent to oil development; rather, they wrestle simultaneously with the promise of oil-based prosperity and the adverse health effects it causes. This Janus-faced existence is beautifully rendered by geographer Gabriela Valdivia whose ethnographic work is situated in the refining port city of Esmeraldas, Ecuador. The stories of the residents living adjacent to the city's refinery, suggest they are "stuck with oil" – to refashion the apt descriptor Córdoba Azcárate (2020) gives to tourism – while they try to secure a "dignified life" in the nation's petropolis (Valdivia 2018).

Conclusion

Since the first half of the nineteenth century, fossil fuels have expanded the spatial scale of urbanization and fundamentally changed the way we inhabit cities. City boosters, state officials, and private investors, by extracting and distributing fossil fuels – especially oil – unleashed exponential growth, entrenched ever-greater production, and, in the process, fully globalized urban metabolisms. Oil has become the economic, social, and political lifeblood of cities and the reason for an entire constellation of technical infrastructures and interconnected urbanized spaces at a planetary scale. The interpretation of the making of this global petroleumscape – in all its physical, economic, and cultural aspects – that I have provided here evinces how challenging it will be to undo. Capital flows, deeply ingrained neocolonial economic relations, and entire urban landscapes and ways of life depend on free-flowing oil and the mass consumption of it. So many of us, tethered to this global petroleumscape, have become dependent on this one commodity and a plethora of other products that would not exist without it. Given ongoing climate destabilization from fossil fuel combustion, alternatives to our oil-saturated way of life are necessary for human existence on our planet. Fortunately for us, those alternatives, which I will discuss in the conclusion, are also possible.

Conclusion

This Element employs a global geographical scale for understanding the histor-ical formation of urban environments, forged by a multiplicity of human and nonhuman actors within the large-scale structural forces of empire, capitalism, and nation-state formation. I contend that this global register brings urban-environmental governance, urban disease ecologies, urban metabolisms, and fossil-based urbanism into sharper relief. At the same time it yields a more refined comparative basis for understanding local variations, contingent on the interplay between sociopolitical formations and ecological conditions (Nightingale 2016). This is not to say that a global register is a prerequisite for doing all urban environmental history; there are some processes and many time periods that can best be understood through more narrow spatial scales. Yet much of the intellectual purchase of global frameworks stems not only from tracing flows and connections but also from understanding how those same flows and connections create an integrated world undergoing similar transform-ations (Conrad 2015). Where appropriate, therefore, local variation must be scrutinized within these globally patterned transformations rather than viewed in isolation. For example, the environmental governance of colonial Hong Kong cannot be fully comprehended without a wider lens that looks at the simultan-eous state strategies and scientific debates taking place in England, or elsewhere around the colonized world. Similarly, the oil infrastructure and urban built environment connecting Lake Maracaibo to Caracas in Venezuela assumes greater meaning as part of a much larger petroleumscape of capital investment, urban energy metabolisms, logistical infrastructures, and petroleum cultures.

Such a scaling-up, ironically, also clarifies the smaller scale – that which is idiosyncratic, reimagined, and divergent.

Here I have sketched out two global histories: that of urban metabolisms made possible by the adoption of fossilized energy and that of urban-environmental governance founded on technocratic practice, environmental conquest, and the racialization of society. This Element is an invitation to scholars to further research these global processes and other related urban-environmental themes. Such themes might include the struggles and negotiations over the transformation of urban aquatic environments or those over environmental sanitation within the context of racialized forms of liberal and colonial governance. Likewise, researchers might explore the working conditions and occupational health of the global petroleumscape and the popular political cultures of petroleum. Or, they might examine the rise of twentieth-century urban environmentalisms, spawned by a mixture of social movements and various forms of technocratic urbanism. Urban disaster histories, like the ones noted in the introduction, but also others, such as heat waves and hurricanes that are becoming more fatal and devastating with rising global temperatures, need greater attention as well.

We also need more locally grounded histories that better situate global urban-environmental phenomena within conventionally understood urban spaces – the municipality, the specific urban ecosystem and its built environment. While this Element has drawn on many local studies, a more fine-grained understanding of the flows and exchanges that have led to global patterns of urban-environmental governance and energy regimes over time remains fundamental. Lest this concluding exploration fall into a trap of abstraction, I will take the case of Mexico City, drawing on a number of recent works, to illustrate these assertions (Perló Cohen 1999; Agostoni 2003; Robertson 2012; Vitz 2018).

During the second half of the nineteenth century, Mexico shared with nations such as Japan, Italy, Germany, and the United States a trajectory of liberal national consolidation, and Mexican elites, like their brethren elsewhere, spearheaded modernization. A cadre of engineers, and later architects and planners, participated in global discussions about urban health, water management, and forestry and established educational institutions at home. Many of these professionals filled the ranks of what became known as the *científicos*, the small clique of technocrats adherent to the authoritarian Porfirio Díaz regime. They built the city's water supply network and its drainage and sewer infrastructure, crafted the city's health codes, developed new subdivisions, and began to regulate its surrounding forestland in ways that broadly fit the mold of the urban-environmental imaginary I outlined in section one.

Yet Mexico City possessed two rather unique political-ecological conditions. First, the city, which in 1910 reached 500,000 inhabitants, was located in a closed, high-altitude basin whose heavy summer rainy season created a series of lakes on the lowest lands adjacent to the city. Lake Texcoco, the lowest-lying of them, would swell after heavy rainstorms and inundate the city. Colonial and postcolonial drainage infrastructure reduced flooding but also desiccated the land. Because saline minerals washed down from the mountains above and settled in the lakebed, desiccation also proved to be deleterious, causing dust storms to rise from the barren, salt-encrusted land (see Figure 3).

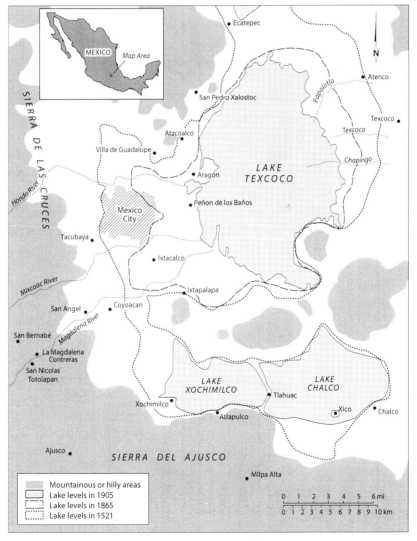

Figure 3 Mexico City and its Surroundings. Courtesy of Bill Nelson

Urban experts around the globe regularly grappled with hydrological dilemmas, but rarely were these questions as existential as they were in Mexico City.

Second, in 1910 the Mexican Revolution, a heterogeneous set of rebellions and violent conflicts that mostly beset the countryside, began, and revolutionaries challenged Mexico's authoritarian and technocratic urban political structures. Although it would be wrong to claim the revolution erupted because of urban-environmental demands, popular classes and reformers made claims to the lands and waters that were integral to the city's metabolism during the era of Porfirio Díaz. These political-ecological conditions marked the ways that city authorities represented the nature of the Basin of Mexico and the ways they sought to control and govern it.

The transformations of Lake Texcoco and the Basin of Mexico's hydrology bring into focus the interplay between the local and the global. The hydraulic engineers that designed the city's Great Drainage Canal, completed in 1900, aimed to prevent flooding, control disease, and open up new lands for urban development and farming. The massive hydraulic project that took several decades to complete fit the mold of the larger global impetus to conquer and control the flow of water within and without cities, but experts in Mexico City knew enough about the hydrology of the basin, specifically its susceptibility to unhealthy desiccation, to ensure that the lake would not completely disappear. Nonetheless, the lake receded, exposing thousands of hectares of barren saline land, and the dust storms, increasingly frequent and large, brought on respiratory illnesses, spoiled market foods, and decreased visibility. These events captured the urban public's imagination and led many urbanists to question the intelligence of the city's drainage infrastructure. The peasant communities that rimmed the old lakebed, however, had other ideas. The nation's agrarian reform turned these residents of the immediate hinterland toward agricultural production, a beacon of hope in a drying environment, and the reformist administration of Lázaro Cárdenas, who was a strong advocate of forest protection, did not embrace the recuperation of the basin's major lake. Instead, he approved an agricultural fertilization project that officials believed would simultaneously defeat the dust storms and satisfy the agricultural needs of campesinos along the lake's edges. Success hinged on the capacity to rid the lakebed of its growth-impairing salts. While this project was unique to Mexico City's political ecology, there were broadly similar iterations wherever rural productivism, state engineering capacity, and political reformism intersected.

The salts proved inveterate and the engineering aims hubristic. The project met its demise in the 1940s, and as urban settlement spread out over the dried lakebed, the dust storms turned more dangerous. The Lake Texcoco problem, as it was known to urban experts, symbolized the larger environmental woes of the fast-growing metropolis. Urban experts witnessed not only tormenting dust storms but also the grave menace of flooding, land subsidence, chronic water shortages, and forest depletion. Mexico City seemed to be a paradox, suffering simultaneously from too little water and too much water. An influential group of scientists, planners, engineers, and architects during the late 1940s and 1950s articulated in essays, editorials, novels, and scientific papers an ecological understanding of Mexico City's condition, emphasizing the dual and interconnected ways that human artifice (namely engineering) and the biophysical properties of the city made environmental problems. A leading architect Guillermo Zárraga (1958: 29) put it best: "The different issues that constitute the problem of the [Basin] of Mexico are interconnected in such a way that one cannot refer to one of them without alluding to the rest. Water and subsidence, for example, are intimately united . . . . Deforestation, erosion, and dust storms are other threads of the same warp."

These urban-ecological ideas, however, were not formed in isolation. They certainly owed to the long history of Mexican technicians and urbanists dealing with the unique hydrology and topology of the Basin of Mexico. But these urbanists also participated in a global intellectual network of scientists and conservationists such as William Vogt and Paul Sears, both of whom visited Mexico City in the 1940s and studied the environmental conditions of its lakebeds. Whereas Vogt and others, such as Henry Fairfield Osborn Jr., used what they learned in their tour of Latin America to advance a Cold War–driven environmentalism that stressed the dangers Malthusian overpopulation and resource crunches posed to national security, their Mexican counterparts applied a decidedly urban lens to create an unlikely urban environmentalism in a rapidly industrializing city. Problems that were once conceived in isolation from one another and as fundamentally about public health became interwoven, and mutually reinforcing, threats to ecological equilibrium requiring integral environmental governance.

As this short exploration of Mexico City's historical environment shows, urban environmental historians must not abandon the localized geographic scales that have heretofore dominated the field. Considerations of urban ecosystems, built environments, and the environmental aspects of urban political culture will always matter. Moreover, the dearth of city-specific and metropolitan environmental histories in areas outside the United States, Canada, and Western Europe is glaring. It is important, nonetheless, that historians avoid the tunnel vision that blinds us to the global integration of urban ecologies.

This global framing of urban environmental history gives us the tools with which to understand the nature of many of our most pressing urban predicaments. Ongoing urban-driven processes of resource extraction and commodification bring ever-greater numbers of nonhuman species into contact with humans, making the evolution of deadly viruses, like the new coronavirus (COVID-19) that emerged in Wuhan, China, in 2019, more likely. And, given the interconnectivity of our most populated cities, a process that intensified about 200 years ago (and has yet to abate), any highly contagious and deadly virus will, most likely, break quarantines and cause a global pandemic. Once circulating in our cities, racist and class-based power structures, if left standing, would again leave black and brown people more susceptible to acute illness and death. Meanwhile, we are facing heat waves, droughts, fires, floods, and sea level rise that will only worsen with more fossil fuel combustion. A new urban imagination, one that aspires to more just and democratic urban ecologies, might very well be our greatest task of the twenty-first century.

Such a political imagination hinges on urgent climate action that can simultaneously address unequal urban power relations. A just climate transition must tackle the interconnected petroleumscape that creates environmental injustice and precarity, on the one hand, and ideas of freedom, material prosperity by means of endless growth, and the promise of redistribution, on the other. To dismantle the global petroleumscape in time to prevent catastrophic climate breakdown, it is unlikely that national policies emphasizing technological breakthroughs, tax incentives, and corporate subsidies will be enough. These policies will certainly not be enough to construct a more democratic, anti-racist, and sustainable world.

Social movements for climate justice in the cities of greatest fossil fuel consumption must seek to build a politics espousing labor rights and the urban commons – of public spaces free of police surveillance, urban density, as well as free and affordable housing, transport, and urban services – that can unite diverse working peoples around electrification, in which solar and wind energy can be prioritized. Such a program to decommodify our lives would also help us kick our unending growth addiction. Our addiction to growth stems, in part, from our primary need to obtain a job that can allow us to sustain ourselves through market relations and consume a seemingly never-ending assortment of goods and services. But unending growth degrades the natural environments upon which we depend and raises the probability that new and deadly viruses will emerge. For example, even if, in theory, technological breakthroughs in solar, wind, and battery storage capacity could support capitalist growth in ways similar to fossil fuels, these "green" technologies require vast expanses of land and precious mineral resources such as cobalt and lithium. A new urban commons, and a broader decommodification of life, would surely reduce the urban metabolism that historically expanded alongside market relations and fossil fuel–driven industrial capitalism. Nonetheless, urban energy metabolisms across vast hinterland spaces would no doubt continue. Therefore, urban-oriented climate movements must foreground coalition building across regional and global hinterlands that can submit energy to a regional commons governance structure, one that redresses centuries of dispossession of Indigenous and farmer lands, protects remaining wildlands, and seeks to suture long-standing metabolic rifts.

This coalitional politics, it appears increasingly likely, will also need to directly challenge the physical petroleumscape through which oil flows and profits are made. The strike, the working classes' primary source of power over fossil capital, may be one possibility, although most workers directly tied to petroleum investment, are unlikely to unite in a call for its demise. Other forms of direct action along the petroleumscape are necessary and possible sources of political leverage. Indeed, the Dakota Access Pipeline (DAPL) protesters at Standing Rock, South Dakota, by chaining themselves to bulldozers, have already proved the potential of such direct actions to stop new fossil fuel infrastructure and cut off the flow of oil (Cowen 2020; Paulo de Rosa 2022). The politics of a just climate transition, therefore, must articulate an alternative to all aspects of the global petroleumscape – its physical infrastructure, the expectations and promises of privatized prosperity it generates, and its financial flows across global space, from the ports and refineries to the extraction zones.

References

Abu-Lughod, Janet L. (1991). *Before European Hegemony: The World System, A.D. 1250–1350*. Oxford: Oxford University Press.

Acker, Antoine. (2020). A Different Story in the Anthropocene: Brazil's Post-colonial Quest for Oil (1930–1975). *Past & Present* 249, 1: 167–211.

Adamson, Michael R. (2018). *Oil and Urbanization on the Pacific Coast: Ralph Bramel Lloyd and the Shaping of the Urban West*. Morgantown: West Virginia University Press.

Agostoni, Claudia. (2003). *Monuments of Progress: Modernization and Public Health in Mexico City, 1876–1910*. Calgary: University of Calgary Press.

Allen, Barbara L. (2006). The Making of Cancer Alley: A Historical View of Louisiana's Chemical Corridor. In Donal Davis and Mark R. Stoll eds. *Southern United States: An Environmental History*. Santa Barbara: ABC-CLIO: 295–301.

Allen, Robert C. (2014). *The British Industrial Revolution in Global Perspective*. Cambridge: Cambridge University Press.

Al-Nakib, Farah. (2015). *Kuwait Transformed: A History of Oil and Urban Life*. Stanford: Stanford University Press.

Anderson, Warwick. (2006). *Colonial Pathologies: American Tropical Medicine, Race, and Hygiene in the Philippines*. Durham: Duke University Press.

Angelo, Hillary and Wachsmuth, David. (2015). Urbanizing Urban Political Ecology: A Critique of Methodological Cityism. *International Journal of Urban and Regional Research* 39, 1: 16–27.

Aparecida Lopes, Maria. (2021). *Rio de Janeiro in the Global Meat Market, c. 1850 to c. 1930: How Fresh and Salted Meat Arrived at the Carioca Table*. New York: Routledge.

Appel, Hannah. (2012). Walls and White Elephants: Oil Extraction, Responsibility, and Institutional Violence in Equatorial Guinea. *Ethnography* 13, 4: 439–465.

Appel, Hannah, Mason, Arthur, and Watts, Michael eds. (2015). *Subterranean Estates Life Worlds of Oil and Gas*. Ithaca: Cornell University Press.

Armiero, Marco. (2017). Migrants in the American Landscape. In Marco Armiero and Richard P. Tucker eds. *Environmental History of Modern Migrations*. London: Routledge Press: 53–75.

Armiero, Marco and Tucker, Richard. (2017). *Environmental History of Modern Migrations*. New York: Routledge Press.

Arnold, David. (1993). *Colonizing the Body: State Medicine and Epidemic Disease in Nineteenth-century India*. Berkeley: University of California Press.

Atabaki, Touraj. (2018). Indian Migrant Workers in the Iranian Oil Industry, 1908–1951. In Touraj Atabaki, Elisabetta Bini, and Kaveh Ehsani eds. *Working for Oil: Comparative Social Histories of Labor in the Global Oil Industry*. London: Palgrave Macmillan: 189–226.

Auyero, Javier and Alejandra Swinstun, Débora. (2009). *Flammable: Environmental Suffering in an Argentine Shantytown*. Oxford: Oxford University Press.

Baer, James. (1998). Buenos Aires: Housing Reform and the Decline of the Liberal State in Argentina. In Ron F. Pineo and James Baer eds. *Cities of Hope: People, Protests, and Progress in Urbanizing Latin America, 1870–1930*. Boulder: Westview Press: 89–129.

Bartolini, Francesco. (2023). Historicizing Urban Informality: An Opportunity to Rethink the Study of the Contemporary City. In Maria Vittoria Ferroni, Rossana Galdini, and Giovanni Ruocco eds. *Urban Informality: A Multidisciplinary Perspective*. Switzerland: Springer: 107–116.

Beckert, Sven. (2014). *Empire of Cotton: A Global History*. New York: Alfred A. Knoph.

Bennett, Jane. (2010). *Vibrant Matter: A Political Ecology of Things*. Durham: Duke University Press.

Bernhardt, Christoph. (2011). At the Limits of the European Sanitary City: Water-Related Environmental Inequalities in Berlin-Brandenburg, c. 1900–1939. In Genevieve Massard-Guilbaud and Richard Rodger eds. *Environmental and Social Justice in the City: Historical Perspectives*. Cambridgeshire: White Horse Press.

Bhattacharyya, Debjani. (2018). *Empire and Ecology in the Bengal Delta: The Making of Calcutta*. Cambridge: Cambridge University Press.

Biggs, David. (2010). *Quagmire: Nation-building and Nature in the Mekong Delta*. Seattle: University of Washington Press.

Bittner, Stephen V. (1998). Green Cities and Orderly Streets: Space and Culture in Moscow, 1928–1933. *Journal of Urban History* 25, 1: 22–56.

Black, Brian C. (2021). *Crude Reality: Petroleum in World History*. Lanham: Rowman and Littlefield.

Blackbourn, David. (2006). *The Conquest of Nature: Water, Landscape, and the Making of Modern Germany*. London: J. Cape.

Blau, Eve. (2018). *Baku: Oil and Urbanism*. Zurich: Park Books.

Boland, Alana. (2016). From Factory to Field: Wastewater Irrigation in China's Early Socialist Cities. *Global Environment* 9: 219–239.

Bolster, Jeffrey. (2014). *The Mortal Sea: Fishing the Atlantic in the Age of Sail*. Cambridge, MA: Belknap Press.

Booth, Douglas E. (1985). Municipal Socialism and City Government Reform: The Milwaukee Experience, 1910–1940. *Journal of Urban History* 12, 1: 51–84.

Booth, Rodrigo. (2013). El Camino como aventura. El automóvil y la movilidad turística en el Chile de comienzos del siglo XX. *Ciudad y Arquitectura* 151: 17–21.

Boughton, John. (2018). *Municipal Dreams: The Rise and Fall of Council Housing*. London: Verso Press.

Brannstrom, Christian. (2005). Was Brazilian Industrialisation Fuelled by Wood? Evaluating the Wood Hypothesis, 1900–1960. *Environment and History* 11, 4: 395–430.

Brenner, Neil J. ed. (2014). *Implosions/Explosions: Towards a Study of Planetary Urbanization*. Berlin: Jovis.

Broich, John. (2007). Engineering the Empire: British Water Supply Systems and Colonial Societies, 1850–1900. *Journal of British Studies* 46, 2: 346–365.

Browning, Elizabeth G. (2022). *Nature's Laboratory: Environmental Thought and Labor Radicalism in Chicago, 1886–1937*. Baltimore: Johns Hopkins University Press.

Buchenau, Jurgen and Johnson, Lyman L. (2009). *Aftershocks: Earthquakes and Popular Politics in Latin America*. Albuquerque: University of New Mexico Press.

Buckley, Eve E. (2017). *Technocrats and the Politics of Drought and Development in Brazil*. Chapel Hill: UNC Press.

Candiani, Vera. (2014). *Dreaming of Dry Land: Environmental Transformation in Colonial Mexico City*. Stanford: Stanford University Press.

Carroll, John M. (2005). *Edge of Empires: Chinese Elites and British Colonials in Hong Kong*. Cambridge, MA: Harvard University Press.

Chakrabarti, Pratik. (2015). Purifying the River: Pollution and Purity of Water in Colonial Calcutta. *Studies in History* 31, 2: 178–205.

Chalhoub, Sidney. (1996). *Cidade Febril: Corticos e epidemias na corte imperial*. Sao Paulo: Companhia das Letras.

Chatterjee, Partha. (2004). *The Politics of the Governed: Reflections on Popular Politics in Most of the World*. New York: Columbia University Press.

Chatterjee, Partha. (1993). *The Nation and Its Fragments: Colonial and Postcolonial Histories*. Princeton: Princeton University Press.

Chattopadhyay, Swati. (2005). *Representing Calcutta: Modernity, Nationalism, and the Colonial Uncanny*. London: Routledge Press.

Chhabria, Sheetal. (2019). *Making the Modern Slum: The Power of Capital in Colonial Bombay*. Seattle: University of Washington.

Chu, Cecilia L. (2013). Combatting Nuisance: Sanitation, Regulation, and the Politics of Property in Colonial Hong Kong. In Robert Peckham and David M. Pomfret eds. *Imperial Contagions: Medicine, Hygiene, and Cultures of Planning in Asia*. Hong Kong: Hong Kong University Press: 17–36.

Chu, Cecilia L. (2022). *Building Colonial Hong Kong: Speculative Development and Segregation in the Colonial City*. London: Routledge Press.

Cioc, Mark. (2002). *The Rhine: An Eco-biography, 1815–2000*. Seattle: University of Washington Press.

Cleary, Patricia. (1997). Contested Terrain: Environmental Agendas and Settlement Choices in Colonial St. Louis. In Andrew Hurley ed. *Common Fields: An Environmental History of St. Louis*. St. Louis: Missouri Historical Society Press: 58–72.

Coen, Deborah R. (2013). *The Earthquake Observers: Disaster Science from Lisbon to Richter*. Chicago: University of Chicago Press.

Conrad, Sebastian. (2015). *What Is Global History?* Princeton: Princeton University Press.

Cooke, Jason. (2017). Energy Landscape: Los Angeles Harbor and the Establishment of Oil-based Capitalism in Southern California, 1871–1930. *Planning Perspectives* 32, 1: 67–86

Coplen, Amy K. (2018). The Labor between Farm and Table: Cultivating an Urban Political Ecology of Agrifood for the 21st Century. *Geography Compass*. 12, 5: 1–12.

Córdoba Azcárate, Matilde. (2020). *Stuck with Tourism: Space, Power, and Labor in Contemporary Yucatán*. Berkeley: University of California Press.

Cornea, Natasha Lee, Véron, Rene, and Zimmer, Anna. (2017). Everyday Governance and Urban Environments: Towards a More Interdisciplinary Urban Political Ecology. *Geography Compass*. 11, 4: 1–12.

Coronil, Fernando. (1997). *The Magical State: Nature, Money, and Modernity in Venezuela*. Chicago: University of Chicago Press.

Cowen, Deborah. (2020). Following the Infrastructures of Empire: Notes on Cities, Settler Colonialism, and Method. *Urban Geography* 41, 4: 469–486.

Crawford, Christina E. (2022). *Spatial Revolution: Architecture and Planning in the Early Soviet Union*. Ithaca: Cornell University Press.

Cronon, William C. (1983). *Changes in the Land: Indians, Colonists, and the Ecology of New England*. New York: Hill and Wang.

Cronon, William C. (1991). *Nature's Metropolis: Chicago and the Great West*. New York: W.W. Norton Press.

Crosby, Alfred. (2004). *Ecological Imperialism: The Biological Expansion of Europe, 900–1900.* Cambridge: Cambridge University Press.

Crossley, Pamela Kyle. (2008). *What Is Global History?* Cambridge, MA: Polity Press.

Curtin, Philip D. (1985). Medical Knowledge and Urban Planning in Tropical Africa. *American Historical Review* 90, 3: 594–613.

Dagenais, Michele and Castonguay, Stephane eds. (2011). *Metropolitan Natures: Environmental Histories of Montreal.* Pittsburgh: University of Pittsburgh Press.

Davis, Diana K. (2007). *Resurrecting the Granary of Rome: Environmental History and French Colonial Expansion in North Africa.* Athens: University of Ohio Press.

Davis, Diane E. (2005). Cities in Global Context: A Brief Intellectual History. *International Journal of Urban and Regional Research* 29, 1: 92–109.

Delgado Ramos, Gian Carlo. (2015). Water and the Political Ecology of Urban Metabolism: The Case of Mexico City. *Journal of Political Ecology* 22, 1: 98–114.

Dogliani, Patrizia. (2002). European Municipalism in the First Half of the Twentieth Century: The Socialist Network. *Contemporary European History* 11, 4: 573–596.

Downs, Jim. (2021). *Maladies of Empire: How Colonialism, Slavery, and War Transformed Empire.* Cambridge: Cambridge University Press.

D'Souza, Rohan. (2008). Framing India's Hydraulic Crises: The Politics of the Modern Large Dam. *Monthly Review* 60, 3: 112–124.

Duffy, John. (1990). *The Sanitarians: A History of American Public Health.* Urbana: University of Illinois Press.

Dyl, Joanna. (2017). *Seismic City an Environmental History of San Francisco's 1906 Earthquake.* Seattle: University of Washington Press.

Dyl, Joanna. (2006). The War on Rats versus the Right to Keep Chickens: Plague and the Paving of San Francisco, 1907–1908. In Andrew C. Isenberg ed. *The Nature of Cities.* Rochester, NY: Rochester University Press: 38–61.

Echenberg, Myron J. (2007). *Plague Ports: The Urban Impact of Bubonic Plague, 1894–1901.* New York: NYU Press.

Edensor, Tim and Jayne, Mark. (2012). Introduction: Urban Theory beyond the West. In Mark Jayne ed. *Urban Theory beyond the West: A World of Cities.* London: New York: Routledge Press: 1-28.

Elling, Christian. (2015). On Lines and Fences: Labor, Community, and Violence in an Oil City. In Ulrike Freitag ed. *Urban Violence in the Middle East: Changing Cityscapes in the Transformation from Empire to Nation State.* New York: Berghahn Books: 197–221.

Estabrook, Thomas, Levenstein, Charles, and Wooding, John. (2018). *Labor-Environmental Coalitions: Lessons from a Louisiana Petrochemical Region*. London: Routledge Press.

Fanon, Frantz. (2004). *The Wretched of the Earth*. Trans Richard Philcox. New York: Grove Press.

Fee, Elizabeth and Brown, Theodore M. eds. (1997). *Making Medical History: The Life and Times of Henry E. Sigerist*. Baltimore: Johns Hopkins University Press.

Fischer, Brodwyn. (2022). Slavery, Freedom, and the Relational City in Abolition-Era Recife. In Brodwyn Fischer and Keila Grinberg eds. *The Boundaries of Freedom: Slavery, Abolition, and the Making of Modern Brazil*. Cambridge: Cambridge University Press: 183–212.

Fischer, Brodwyn. (2014). A Century in the Present Tense: Crisis, Politics, and the Intellectual History of Brazil's Informal Cities. In Brodwyn Fischer, Bryan McCann and Javier Auyero eds. *Cities from Scratch: Poverty and Informality in Urban Latin America*. Durham: Duke University Press: 9–67.

Fogelson, Robert M. (2022). *Working-Class Utopias: A History of Cooperative Housing in New York City*. Princeton: Princeton University Press.

Foster, John Bellamy. (1999). Marx's Theory of Metabolic Rift: Classical Foundations for Environmental Sociology. *The American Journal of Sociology* 105, 2: 366-405.

French, R. E. and Hamilton, F. E. Ian eds. (1979). *The Socialist City: Spatial Structure and Urban Policy*. New York: Wiley.

Fucarro, Nelida. (2022). Arab Oil Towns as Petrohistories. In Carola Hein ed. *Oil Spaces: Exploring the Global Petroleumscape*. London: Routledge Press: 129–144.

Fuccaro, Nelida. (2015). Reading Oil as Urban Violence: Kirkuk and Its Oil Conurbation, 1927–1958. In Ulrike Freitag ed. *Urban Violence in the Middle East: Changing Cityscapes in the Transformation from Empire to Nation State*. New York: Berghahn Books: 222–242.

Fucarro, Nelida. (2009). *Histories of City and State in the Persian Gulf: Manama since 1800*. Cambridge: Cambridge University Press.

Gandy, Matthew. (2008). Landscapes of Disaster: Water, Modernity, and Urban Fragmentation in Mumbai. *Environment and Planning A: Economy and Space* 40, 1: 108–130.

Gandy, Matthew. (2006). Planning, Anti-planning and the Infrastructure Crisis Facing Metropolitan Lagos. *Urban Studies* 43, 2: 371–396.

Gandy, Matthew. (2002). *Concrete and Clay: Reworking Nature in New York City*. Cambridge, MA: MIT Press.

Ghosh, Nabaparna. (2022). *A Hygienic City-Nation: Space, Community, and Everyday Life in Colonial Calcutta*. Cambridge: Cambridge University Press.

Ghrawi, Claudia. (2015). Structural and Physical Violence in Saudi Arabian Oil Towns, 1953–1956. In Ulrike Freitag ed. *Urban Violence in the Middle East: Changing Cityscapes in the Transformation from Empire to Nation State*. New York: Berghahn Books: 243–264.

Gilbert, Pamela K. (2002). The Victorian Social Body and Urban Cartography. In Pamela K. Gilbert ed. *Imagined Londons*. Albany: SUNY Press: 11–30.

Gill, G., Burrell, S., and Brown, J. (2001). Fear and Frustration — the Liverpool Cholera Riots of 1832. *The Lancet* 358, 9227: 233–237.

Gitlin, Jay, Berglund, Barbara., and Arenson, Adam. eds. (2013). *Frontier Cities: Encounters at the Crossroads of Empire*. Philadelphia: University of Pennsylvania Press.

Goebel, Michael. (2015). *Anti-Imperial Metropolis: Interwar Paris and the Seeds of Third World Nationalism*. New York: Cambridge University Press.

Gorman, Hugh S. (2007). The Houston Ship Canal and the Changing Landscape of Industrial Pollution. In Martin V. Melosi and Joseph Pratt eds. *Energy Metropolis: An Environmental History of Houston and the Gulf Coast*. Pittsburgh: University of Pittsburgh Press: 52–68.

Graeber, David and Wengrow, David. (2021). *The Dawn of Everything: A New History of Humanity*. New York: Farrar, Straus and Giroux.

Haderer, Margaret. (2023). *Rebuilding Cities and Citizens: Mass Housing in Red Vienna and Cold War Berlin*. Amsterdam: Amsterdam University Press.

Hanley, Susan B. (1987). Urban Sanitation in Preindustrial Japan. *The Journal of Interdisciplinary History* 18: 1–26.

Harper, Sam. (2007). Did Clean Water Reduce Black-White Mortality Inequalities in the United States. *International Journal of Epidemiology* 36: 248–257.

Harrison, Mark. (2013). *Contagion: How Commerce Has Spread Disease*. New Haven: Yale University Press.

Healey, Mark. (2011). *Ruins of the New Argentina: Peronism and the Remaking of San Juan after the 1944 Earthquake*. Durham: Duke University Press.

Hein, Carola. (2022). Space, Time, and Oil: The Global Petroleumscape. In Carola Hein ed. *Oil Spaces: Exploring the Global Petroleumscape*. London: Routledge Press: 3–18.

Hein, Carola. (2018). Oil Spaces: The Global Petroleumscape in the Rotterdam/The Hague Area. *Journal of Urban History* 44, 5: 887–929.

Hein, Carola. (2010). Global Landscapes of Oil. In Rania Ghosn ed. *New Geographies II: Landscapes of Energy.* Cambridge, MA: Harvard University Press: 33-42.

Henry, Todd A. (2014). *Assimilating Seoul: Japanese Rule and the Politics of Public Space in Colonial Korea, 1910–1945.* Berkeley: University of California Press.

Heynen, Nik. (2016). Urban Political Ecology II: The Abolitionist Century. *Progress in Human Geography* 40, 6: 839–845.

Heynen, Nik. (2014). Urban Political Ecology I: The Urban Century. *Progress in Human Geography* 38, 4: 598–604.

Heynen, Nik, Kaika, Maria, and Swyngedouw, Eric. (2006). *In the Nature of Cities: Urban Political Ecology and the Politics of Urban Metabolism.* London: Routledge Press.

Hill, Christopher. (2013). Conceptual Universalization in the Transnational Nineteenth Century. In Samuel Moyn and Andrew Sartori eds. *Global Intellectual History.* New York: Columbia University Press: 134–158.

Hirst, Paul W. (2012). *The Wired Northwest: The History of Electric Power, 1870s–1970s.* Lawrence: University of Kansas Press.

Hoffman, David L. (1994). *Peasant Metropolis: Social Identities in Moscow, 1929–1941.* Ithaca: Cornell University Press.

Hosagrahar, Jyoti. (2005). *Indigenous Modernities: Negotiating Architecture and Urbanism.* New York: Routledge Press.

Hossain, Mohammad. (2021). Colonial Infrastructure, Ecology, and Epidemics in Dhaka, 1858–1947. In Mohammad Gharipour and Caitlin DeClercq eds. *Epidemic Urbanism: Contagious Diseases in Global Cities.* Chicago: Intellect, University of Chicago Press: 188–194.

Hou, Li. (2018). *Building for Oil: Daqing and the Formation of the Chinese Socialist State.* Cambridge, MA: Harvard University Press.

Huber, Matthew. (2013). *Lifeblood: Oil, Freedom and the Forces of Capital.* Minneapolis: University of Minnesota Press.

Hundley Jr., Norris. (1992). *The Great Thirst: Californians and Water, 1770s–1990s.* Berkeley: University of California Press.

Hungerford, Hillary and Smiley, Sarah L. (2016). Comparing Colonial Water Provision in British and French Africa. *Journal of Historical Geography* 52: 74–83.

Jafari, Peyman. (2018). *Fluid History: Oil Workers and the Iranian Revolution.* In Touraj Atabaki, Elisabetta Bini, and Kaveh Ehsani eds. *Working for Oil: Comparative Social Histories of Labor in the Global Oil Industry.* London: Palgrave Macmillan: 69–98.

Jennings, Eric T. (2006). *Curing the Colonizers: Hydrotherapy, Climatology, and French Colonial Spas*. Durham: Duke University Press.

Jiménez, Christina M. (2019). *Making an Urban Public: Popular Claims to the City in Mexico, 1879–1932*. Pittsburgh: University of Pittsburgh Press.

Jones, Christopher F. (2014). *Routes of Power: Energy and Modern America*. Cambridge, MA: Harvard University Press.

Joyce, Patrick. (2003). *The Rule of Freedom: Liberalism and the Modern City*. New York: Verso Press.

Kagan, Richard. (2000). *Urban Images of the Hispanic World, 1493–1793*. Stanford: Stanford University Press.

Kaika, Maria. (2005). *City of Flows: Modernity, Nature, and the City*. London: Routledge Press.

Kawa, Nicolas C. (2019). Night Soil: Origins, Discontinuities, and Opportunities for Bridging the Metabolic Rift. *Ethnobiology Letters* 10, 1: 40–9.

Kelman, Ari. (2003). *A River and Its City: The Nature of Landscape in New Orleans*. Berkeley: University of California Press.

Kenny, Nicolas and Madgin, Rebecca. (2016). *Cities beyond Borders: Comparative and Transnational Approaches to Urban History*. London: Routledge Press.

Khalili, Laleh. (2020). *Sinews of War and Trade: Shipping and Capitalism in the Arabian Peninsula*. New York: Verso Press.

Kiddle, Amelia M. ed. (2021). *Energy in the Americas: Critical Reflections on Energy and History*. Calgary: University of Calgary Press.

Kim Jessica M. (2019). *Imperial Metropolis: Los Angeles, Mexico, and the Borderlands of American Empire, 1865–1941*. Chapel Hill: UNC Press.

Klingle, Matthew. (2007). *Emerald City: An Environmental History of Seattle*. New Haven: Yale University Press.

Kooy, Michelle, and Bakker, Karen. (2008). Technologies of Government: Constituting Subjectivities, Spaces and Infrastructures in Colonial and Contemporary Jakarta. *International Journal of Urban and Regional Research* 32, 2, 375–391.

Kozlof, Nikolas. (2004). From Lakeshore Village to Oil Boom Town: Lagunillas under Venezuela Dictator Juan Vicente Gómez. In Christian Branstromm ed. *Territories, Commodities, and Knowledges: Latin American Environmental Histories in the Nineteenth and Twentieth Centuries*. London: Institute for the Study of the Americas; 90–118.

Kueker, Glen David. (2008). Public Health, Yellow Fever and the Making of Modern Tampico. *Urban History Review* 36, 2: 18–28.

Kwak, Nancy H. (2015). *A World of Homeowners: American Power and the Politics of Housing Aid*. Chicago: University of Chicago Press.

Lasso, Marixa. (2019). *Erased: The Untold Story of the Panama Canal.* Cambridge, MA: Belknap Press.

Latour, Bruno. (2005). *Reassembling the Social: An Introduction to Actor-Network-Theory.* Oxford: Oxford University Press.

Lee, Paula Young ed. (2008). *Meat, Modernity and the Rise of the Slaughterhouse.* Durham, : University of New Hampshire Press.

Lefebvre, Henri. (2003). *The Urban Revolution* trans. Robert Bononno. Minneapolis: University of Minnesota Press.

Legg, Stephen. (2013). Planning Social Hygiene: From Contamination to Contagion in Interwar India. In Robert Peckham and David M. Pomfret eds. *Imperial Contagions: Medicine, Hygiene, and Cultures of Planning in Asia.* Hong Kong: Hong Kong University Press: 105–122.

Leopold, Les. (2007). *The Man Who Hated Work and Loved Labor.* White River Junction: Chelsea Green.

Libertun de Deren, Nora. (2012). Public Parks in the Americas: New York City and Buenos Aires. In Tim Edensor and Mark Jayne eds. *Urban Theory beyond the West: A World of Cities.* New York: Routledge Press: 111–120.

Logan, Steven. (2021). *In the Suburbs of History: Modernist Visions of the Urban Periphery.* Toronto: University of Toronto Press.

Logan, William S. (2000). *Hanoi: Biography of a City.* Seattle: University of Washington Press.

Malm, Andreas. (2016). *Fossil Capital: The Rise of Steam Power and the Roots of Global Warming.* London: Verso.

Mann, Michael and Sehrawat, Samiksha. (2009). A City with a View: The Afforestation of the Delhi Ridge, 1883–1913. *Modern Asian Studies* 43, 2: 543–570.

Mann, Michael. (2007). Delhi's Belly: On the Management of Water, Sewage and Excreta in a Changing Urban Environment during the Nineteenth Century. *Studies in History* 23, 1: 1–31.

McFarlane, Colin. (2010). The Comparative City: Knowledge, Learning, Urbanism. *International Journal of Urban and Regional Research* 34, 4: 725–742.

McFarlane, Colin. (2008). Governing the Contaminated City: Infrastructure and Sanitation in Colonial and Post-Colonial Bombay. *International Journal of Urban and Regional Research* 32, 2: 415–435.

McNeill, J. R. (2010). *Mosquito Empires: Ecology and War in the Greater Caribbean.* Cambridge, MA: Harvard University Press.

McNeur, Catherine. (2014). *Taming Manhattan: Environmental Battles in the Antebellum City.* Cambridge, MA: Harvard University Press.

Meade, Teresa. (1998). *"Civilizing Rio": Reform and Resistance in a Brazilian City, 1889–1930*. University Park: Penn State University Press.

Meade, Teresa. (1989). Living Worse and Costing More: Resistance and Riot in Rio de Janeiro, 1890–1917. *Journal of Latin American Studies* 21: 241–266.

Melosi, Martin. (2000). *The Sanitary City: Urban Infrastructure in America from Colonial Times to the Present*. Baltimore: Johns Hopkins Press.

Melton, Fredrik. (2019). *Electrical Palestine: Capital and Technology from Empire to Nation*. Oakland: University of California Press.

Merchant, Carolyn. (1989). *Ecological Revolutions: Nature, Gender, and Science in New England*. Chapel Hill: UNC Press.

Miescher, Stephan F. (2012). Building the City of the Future: Visions and Experiences of Modernity in Ghana's Akosombo Township. *Journal of African History* 53, 3: 367–390.

Mikhail, Alan ed. (2012). *Water on Sand: Environmental Histories of the Middle East and North Africa*. New York: Oxford University Press.

Mikhail, Alan. (2017). *Under Osman's Tree: The Ottoman Empire, Egypt, and Environmental History*. Chicago: University of Chicago Press.

Mintz, Sidney W. (1985). *Sweetness and Power: The Place of Sugar in Modern History*. New York: Viking Press.

Mitchell, Timothy. (2011). *Carbon Democracy: Political Power in the Age of Oil*. London: Verso Press.

Mitchell, Timothy. (1988). *Colonising Egypt*. Berkeley: University of California Press.

Molesky, Mark. (2015). *This Gulf of Fire: The Great Lisbon Earthquake, or Apocalypse in the Age of Science and Reason*. New York: Vintage.

Molina, Natalia. (2006). *Fit to Be Citizens?: Public Health and Race in Los Angeles, 1879–1939*. Berkeley: University of California Press.

Montaño, Diana J. (2021). *Electrifying Mexico: Technology and the Transformation of a Modern City*. Austin: University of Texas Press.

Moore, Jason W. (2015). *Capitalism in the Web of Life: Ecology and the Accumulation of Capital*. London: Verso.

Morris, Christopher. (2012). *The Big Muddy: An Environmental History of the Mississippi and Its Peoples from Hernando de Soto to Hurricane Katrina*. Oxford: Oxford University Press.

Mumford, Lewis. (1968). *The City in History: Its Origins, Its Transformations, and Its Prospects*. Boston: Mariner Books.

Nash, Linda. (2006). *Inescapable Ecologies: A History of Environment, Disease, and Knowledge*. Berkeley: University of California Press.

Nash, Linda. (2005). The Agency of Nature or the Nature of Agency. *Environmental History* 10, 1: 67–69.

Needham, Andrew. (2014). *Power Lines: Phoenix and the Making of the Modern Southwest*. Princeton: Princeton University Press.

Nightingale, Carl H. (2022). *Earthopolis: A Biography of Our Urban Planet*. Cambridge: Cambridge University Press.

Nightingale, Carl H. (2016). The Seven Cs: Reflections on Writing a Global History of Urban Segregation. In Nicolas Kenny and Rebecca Madgin eds. *Cities beyond Borders: Comparative and Transnational Approaches to Urban History*. London: Routledge Press: 27–42.

Nightingale, Carl H. (2012). *Segregation: A Global History of Divided Cities*. Chicago: University of Chicago Press.

Nikiforuk, Andrew. (2012). *The Energy of Slaves: Oil and the New Servitude*. Berkeley: Greystone Books.

Njoh, Ambe J. (2012). *Urban Planning and Public Health in Africa: Historical, Theoretical and Practical Dimensions of a Continent's Water and Sanitation Problematic*. New York: Routledge Press.

Odari, Catherine. (2021). Colonialism, Racism, and the Government Response to Bubonic Plague in Nairobi, Kenya, 1895–1910. In Mohammad Gharipour and Caitlin DeClercq eds. *Epidemic Urbanism: Contagious Diseases in Global Cities*. Chicago: Intellect, University of Chicago Press: 75–81.

Olsson, Torre C. (2017). *Agrarian Crossings: Reformers and the Remaking of the US and Mexican Countryside*. Princeton: Princeton University Press.

Otter, Chris. (2017). The Technosphere: A New Concept for Urban Studies. *Urban History* 44, 1: 145–154.

Pande, Ishita. (2010). *Medicine, Race, and Liberalism in British Bengal: Symptoms of Empire*. New York: Routledge Press.

Patel, Raj and Marya, Rupa. (2021). *Inflamed: Deep Medicine and the Anatomy of Injustice*. New York: Farrar, Straus and Giroux.

Patel, Raj and Moore, Jason W. (2017). *A History of the World in Seven Cheap Things: A Guide to Capitalism, Nature, and the Future of the Planet*. Berkeley: University of California Press.

Paulo de Rosa, Salvatore. (2022). Breaking Consensus, Transforming Metabolisms: Notes on Direct-Action against Fossil Fuels through Urban Political Ecology. *Social Text* 40, 150: 135–155.

Pavilack, Jody. (2011). *Mining for the Nation: The Politics of Chile's Coal Communities from the Popular Front to the Cold War*. University Park: Penn State University Press.

Peard, Julyan G. (1999). *Race, Place and Medicine: The Idea of the Tropics in Nineteenth-Century Brazilian Medicine*. Durham: Duke University Press.

Peckham, Robert. (2015). Hygienic Nature: Afforestation and the Greening of Colonial Hong Kong. *Modern Asian Studies 49*, 4: 1177–1209.

Peckham, Robert and Pomfret, David M. (2013). Introduction: Medicine, Hygiene, and the Re-ordering of Empire. In Robert Peckham and David M. Pomfret eds. *Imperial Contagions: Medicine, Hygiene, and Cultures of Planning in Asia*. Hong Kong: Hong Kong University Press: 1–16.

Pelletier, Louis-Raphaël. (2011). The Destruction of the Rural Hinterland: Industrialization of Landscapes in Beauharnois County. In Michele Dagenais and Stephane Castonguay eds. *Metropolitan Natures: Environmental Histories of Montreal*. Pittsburgh: University of Pittsburgh Press: 245–264.

Perló Cohen, Manuel. (2012). *Guerra por el agua en el valle de México?: Estudio sobre las relaciones hidráulicas entre el Distrito Federal y el Estado de México*. Mexico City: UNAM.

Perló Cohen, Manuel. (1999). *El desagüe porfiriano: La historia del desagüe del valle de México*. Mexico City: Porrua.

Peyerl, Drielli. (2022). Building Brazil's Petroleumscape on Land and Sea: Infrastructure, Expertise, and Technology. In Carola Hein ed. *Oil Spaces: Exploring the Global Petroleumscape*. London: Routledge Press: 145–158.

Pilcher, Jeffrey M. (2006). *The Sausage Rebellion: Public Health, Private Enterprise, and Meat in Mexico City, 1890–1917*. Albuquerque: University of New Mexico Press.

Pirani, Simon. (2018). *Burning Up: A Global History of Fossil Fuel Consumption*. London: Pluto Press.

Platt, Harold. (2005). *Shock Cities: The Environmental Transformation and Reform of Manchester and Chicago*. Chicago: University of Chicago Press.

Prashad, Vijay. (2001). The Technology of Sanitation in Colonial Delhi. *Modern Asian Studies* 35, 1: 113–135.

Pratt, Joseph. (2007). A Mixed Blessing: Energy, Economic Growth, and Houston's Environment. In Martin V. Melosi and Joseph Pratt eds. *Energy Metropolis: An Environmental History of Houston and the Gulf Coast*. Pittsburgh: University of Pittsburgh Press: 21–51.

Quam-Wickham, Nancy. (1998). "Cities Sacrificed on the Altar of Oil": Popular Opposition to Oil Development in 1920s Los Angeles. *Environmental History* 3, 2: 189–209.

Rabinow, Paul. (1985). *French Modern: Norms and Forms of the Social Environment*. Chicago: University of Chicago Press.

Rector, Josiah. (2022). *Toxic Debt: An Environmental Justice History of Detroit*. Chapel Hill: UNC Press.

Reinhard, Wolfgang ed. (2015). *Empires and Encounters: 1350–1750*. Cambridge: Belknap Press.

Righter, Robert W. (2005). *The Battle over Hetch-Hetchy: America's Most Controversial Dam and the Birth of Modern Environmentalism*. Oxford: Oxford University Press.

Robbins, Paul. (2012). *Lawn People: How Grasses, Weeds, and Chemicals Make Us Who We Are*. Philadelphia: Temple University Press.

Robertson, Thomas. (2012). *The Malthusian Moment: Global Population Growth and the Birth of American Environmentalism*. New Brunswick: Rutgers University Press.

Robinson, Jennifer. (2006). *Ordinary Cities: Between Modernity and Development*. New York: Routledge Press.

Rodgers, Daniel T. (1998). *Atlantic Crossings: Social Politics in a Progressive Age*. Cambridge: Belknap Press.

Rodgers, Dennis. (2012). An Illness Called Managua: "Extraordinary" Urbanization and "Mal-development" in Nicaragua. In Tim Edensor and Mark Jayne eds. *Urban Theory beyond the West: A World of Cities*. New York: Routledge Press: 134–148

Rogaski, Ruth. (2004). *Hygienic Modernity: Meanings of Health and Disease in Treaty-port China*. Berkeley: University of California Press.

Rome, Adam. (2001). *The Bulldozer in the Countryside: Suburban Sprawl and the Rise of American Environmentalism*. Cambridge: Cambridge University Press.

Ross, Michael L. (2012). *The Oil Curse: How Petroleum Wealth Shapes the Development of Nations*. Princeton: Princeton University Press.

Russell, James M. (1982). Politics, Municipal Services, and the Working Class in Atlanta, 1865–1890. *Georgia Historical Quarterly* 66: 467–491.

Sandoval Strausz, A. K. and Kwak, Nancy H. (2018). *Making Cities Global: The Transnational Turn in Urban History*. Philadelphia: University of Pennsylvania Press.

Santiago, Myrna. (2012). Class and Nature in the Oil Industry of Northern Veracruz, 1900–1938. In Christopher R. Boyer ed. *A Land between Waters: Environmental Histories of Modern Mexico*. Tucson: University of Arizona Press: 173–191.

Santiago, Myrna. (2006). *The Ecology of Oil: Environment, Labor, and the Mexican Revolution*. Cambridge: Cambridge University Press.

Sanzana Calvet, Martin and Castán Broto, Vanesa. (2020). Sacrifice Zones and the Construction of Urban Energy Landscapes in Concepción, Chile. *Journal of Political Ecology* 27, 1: 279–299.

Saunier, Pierre-Yves and Ewen, Shane. (2008). *Another Global City: Historical Explorations into the Transnational Municipal Moment*. New York: Palgrave MacMillan.

Sawyer, Suzana. (2004). *Crude Chronicles: Indigenous Politics, Multinational Oil, and Neoliberalism in Ecuador*. Durham: Duke University Press.

Schmidt, Deanna H. (2017). Suburban Wilderness in the Houston Metropolitan Landscape. *Journal of Political Ecology*. 24, 1: 167–185.

Scott, James C. (2018). *Against the Grain: A Deep History of the Earliest States*. New Haven: Yale University Press.

Scott, James C. (1999). *Seeing Like a State: How Certain Schemes to Improve the Condition Have Failed*. New Haven: Yale University Press.

Seiferle, Rolf Peter and Osmann, Michael P. (2010). *The Subterranean Forest: Energy Systems and the Industrial Revolution*. Cambridgeshire: The White Horse Press.

Sellers, Christopher C. (2015). *Crabgrass Crucible: Suburban Nature and the Rise of Environmentalism in Twentieth-Century America*. Chapel Hill: UNC Press.

Sellers, Christopher C. (2012). Petropolis and Environmental Protest in Cross-National Perspective: Beaumont-Port Arthur, Texas, versus Minatitlan-Coatzacoalcos, Veracruz. *Journal of American History* 99, 1: 111–123.

Sennett, Richard. (1996). *Flesh and Stone: The Body and the City in Western Civilization*. New York: W.W. Norton.

Shah, Nayan. (2001). *Contagious Divides: Epidemics and Race in San Francisco's Chinatown*. Berkeley: University of California Press.

Sheller, Mimi and Urry, John. (2000). The City and the Car. *International Journal of Urban and Regional Research* 24, 4: 737–757.

Shlimon, Arbella Bet. (2019). *City of Black Gold: Oil, Ethnicity, and the Making of Modern Kirkuk*. Stanford: Stanford University Press.

Shlimon, Arbella Bet. (2013). The Politics and Ideology of Urban Development in Iraq's Oil City: Kirkuk, 1946–58. *Comparative Studies of South Asia, Africa, and the Middle East* 33, 1: 26–40.

Shulman, Peter A. (2015). *Coal and Empire: The Birth of Energy Security in Industrial America*. Baltimore: Johns Hopkins University Press.

Sigelbaum, Lewis H. ed. (2012). *The Socialist Car: Automobility in the Eastern Bloc*. Ithaca: Cornell University Press.

Sigelbaum, Lewis H. (2008). *Cars for Comrades: The Life of the Soviet Automobile*. Ithaca: Cornell University Press.

Simpson, Michael. (2022). Fossil Urbanism: Fossil Fuel Flows, Settler Colonial Circulations, and the Production of Carbon Cities. *Urban Geography* 43, 1: 101–122.

Simpson, Michael and Bagelman, Jen. (2018). Decolonizing Urban Political Ecologies: The Production of Nature in Settler Colonial Cities. *Annals of the American Association of Geographers*. 108, 2: 558–568.

Smil, Vaclav. (1994). *Energy in World History.* Boulder: Westview Press.

Smith, David F. and Phillips, Jim eds. (2000). *Food, Science, Politics, and Regulation in the Twentieth Century: International and Comparative Perspectives.* London: Routledge Press.

Stapleton, Kristin. (2022). *The Modern City in Asia.* Elements in Global Urban History. Cambridge: Cambridge University Press.

Steinberg, T. ed. (2002). Down to Earth: Nature, Agency, and Power in History. *American Historical Review* 107, 3: 798–820.

Stradling, David. (1999). *Smokestacks and Progressives: Environmentalists, Engineers, and Air Quality in America, 1881–1951.* Baltimore: Johns Hopkins University Press.

Straeten, Jonas van der. (2016). Connecting the Empire: New Research Perspectives on Infrastructures and the Environment in the (Post) Colonial World. *NTM Zeitschrift für Geschichte der Wissenschaften, Technik und Medizin* 24, 4: 355–391.

Sugrue, Thomas J. "Foreword" (2018). In A. K. Sandoval Strausz and Nancy H. Kwak eds. *Making Cities Global: The Transnational Turn in Urban History.* Philadelphia: University of Pennsylvania Press: vii–x.

Sutoris, Peter. (2016). *Visions of Development: Films Division of India and the Imagination of Progress, 1948–75.* Oxford: Oxford University Press.

Swyngedouw, Eric. (2004). *Social Power and the Urbanization of Water: Flows of Power.* Oxford: Oxford University Press.

Tarr, Joel A. (1996). *The Search for the Ultimate Sink: Urban Pollution in Historical Perspective.* Akron: University of Akron Press.

Tarr, Joel A. (1975). From City to Farm: Urban Wastes and the American Farmer. *Agricultural History* 49, 4: 598–612.

Tenorio Trillo, Mauricio. (1996). *Mexico at the World's Fairs: Crafting a Modern Nation, 1880s–1920s.* Berkeley: University of California Press.

Tinker Salas, Miguel. (2009). *The Enduring Legacy: Oil, Culture, and Society in Venezuela.* Durham: Duke University Press.

Tomes, Nancy. (1998). *The Gospel of Germs: Men, Women, and the Microbe in American Life.* Cambridge, MA: Harvard University Press.

Troesken, Werner. (2004). *Race, Water, and Disease.* Cambridge, MA: MIT Press.

Tsing, Anna L. (2005). *Friction: An Ethnography of Global Connection.* Princeton: Princeton University Press.

Tutino, John. (2007). The Revolutionary Capacity of Rural Communities: Ecological Autonomy and Its Demise. In Elisa Servin, Leticia Reyna, and John Tutino eds. *Cycles of Conflict, Centuries of Change: Crisis, Reform, and Revolution in Mexico.* Durham: Duke University Press: 211–268.

Uekötter, Frank. (2009). *The Age of Smoke: Environmental Policy in Germany and the United States, 1880–1970*. Pittsburgh: University of Pittsburgh Press.

Valdivia, Gabriela and Marcela Benavides. (2018). "The End of the Good Fight?": Organized Labor and the Petro-Nation during the Neoliberalization of the Oil Industry in Ecuador. In Touraj Atabaki, Elisabetta Bini, and Kaveh Ehsani eds. *Working for Oil: Comparative Social Histories of Labor in the Global Oil Industry*. London: Palgrave Macmillan: 159–185.

Valdivia, Gabriela. (2018). "Wagering Life" in the Petro-City: Embodied Ecologies of Oil Flow, Capitalism, and Justice in Esmeraldas, Ecuador. *Annals of the American Association of Geographers* 108, 2: 549–557.

Valenzuela Aguilera, Alfonso. (2014). *Urbanistas y visionarios. La planeación de la ciudad de México en la primera mitad del siglo XX*. Mexico City: Porrúa.

Van Der Geest, Sjak. (2002). The Night Soil Collector: Bucket Latrines in Ghana. *Postcolonial Studies: Culture, Politics, Economy* 5: 197–206.

Vann, Michael. (2021). French Urbanism, Vietnamese Resistance, and the Plague in Hanoi, Vietnam, 1885–1910. In Mohammad Gharipour and Caitlin DeClercq eds. *Epidemic Urbanism: Contagious Diseases in Global Cities*. Chicago: Intellect, University of Chicago Press: 213–221.

Vann, Michael G. and Liz Clarke ill. (2019). *The Great Hanoi Rat Hunt: Empire, Disease, and Modernity in French Colonial Vietnam*. New York: Oxford University Press.

Varlik, Nükhet. (2013). *Plague and Empire in the Early Modern Mediterranean World: The Ottoman Experience, 1347–1600*. New York: Cambridge University Press.

Vergara, Germán. (2021). *Fueling Mexico: Energy and Environment, 1850–1950*. Cambridge: Cambridge University Press.

Vitalis, Robert. (2009). *America's Kingdom: Myth-Making on the Saudi Oil Frontier*. London: Verso Press.

Vitz, Matthew. (2018). *A City on a Lake: Urban Political Ecology and the Growth of Mexico City*. Durham: Duke University Press.

Vorms, Charlotte. (2022). *La Forja del Extrarradio: La Construcción del Madrid Popular (1860–1936)*. Madrid: Editorial Comares.

Walker, Brett L. (2011). *Toxic Archipelago: A History of Industrial Disease in Japan*. Seattle: University of Washington Press.

Washington, Sylvia H. (2005). *Packing Them in: An Archaeology of Environmental Racism in Chicago, 1865–1954*. Lanham: Lexington Books.

Watts, Michael. (2012). A Tale of Two Gulfs: Life, Death, and Dispossession along Two Oil Frontiers. *American Quarterly* 64, 3: 437–467.

Watts, Michael ed. (2008). *Curse of the Black Gold: 50 Years of Oil in the Niger Delta*. Photographs by Ed Kashi. Brooklyn: Powerhouse Books.

Webster, Emily. (2021). Plague, Displacement, and Ecological Disruption in Bombay, India, 1896. In Mohammad Gharipour and Caitlin DeClercq eds. *Epidemic Urbanism: Contagious Diseases in Global Cities*. Chicago: University of Chicago Press: 204–212.

Wells, Christopher W. (2014). *Car Country: An Environmental History*. Seattle: University of Washington Press.

Wolfe, Joel. (2010). *Autos and Progress: The Brazilian Search for Modernity*. Oxford: Oxford University Press.

Xue, Yong. (2005). Treasure Nightsoil as if It Were Gold: Economic and Ecological Links between Urban and Rural Areas in Late Imperial Jiangnan. *Late Imperial China* 26: 41–71.

Yeoh, Brenda S. A. (2013). *Contesting Space in Colonial Singapore: Power Relations and the Urban Built Environment*. Singapore: NUS Press.

Yergin, Daniel. (1991). *The Prize: The Epic Quest for Oil, Money, and Power*. New York: Simon and Shuster.

Young, Kevin. (2015). *Blood of the Earth: Resource Nationalism, Revolution, and Empire in Bolivia*. Austin: University of Texas Press.

Zárraga, Guillermo. (1958). *La tragedia del valle de México*. Mexico City: Stylo.

Zeheter, Michael. (2015). *Epidemics, Empire, and Environments: Cholera in Madras and Quebec City, 1818–1910*. Pittsburgh University of Pittsburgh Press.

Cambridge Elements ≡

Global Urban History

Michael Goebel

Graduate Institute Geneva

Michael Goebel is the Pierre du Bois Chair Europe and the World and Associate Professor of International History at the Graduate Institute Geneva. His research focuses on the histories of nationalism, of cities, and of migration. He is the author of *Anti-Imperial Metropolis: Interwar Paris and the Seeds of Third World Nationalism* (2015).

Tracy Neumann

Wayne State University

Tracy Neumann is an Associate Professor of History at Wayne State University. Her research focuses on global and transnational approaches to cities and the built environment. She is the author of *Remaking the Rust Belt: The Postindustrial Transformation of North America* (2016) and of essays on urban history and public policy.

Joseph Ben Prestel

Freie Universität Berlin

Joseph Ben Prestel is an Assistant Professor (wissenschaftlicher Mitarbeiter) of history at Freie Universität Berlin. His research focuses on the histories of Europe and the Middle East in the nineteenth and twentieth centuries as well as on global and urban history. He is the author of *Emotional Cities: Debates on Urban Change in Berlin and Cairo, 1860–1910* (2017).

About the Series

This series proposes a new understanding of urban history by reinterpreting the history of the world's cities. While urban history has tended to produce single-city case studies, global history has mostly been concerned with the interconnectedness of the world. Combining these two approaches produces a new framework to think about the urban past. The individual titles in the series emphasize global, comparative, and transnational approaches. They deliver empirical research about specific cities, while also exploring questions that expand the narrative outside the immediate locale to give insights into global trends and conceptual debates. Authored by established and emerging scholars whose work represents the most exciting new directions in urban history, this series makes pioneering research accessible to specialists and non-specialists alike.

Cambridge Elements ≡

Global Urban History

Printed in the United States
by Baker & Taylor Publisher Services